DØ197863

This book is based on the Susi Madron organization's very successful 'Cycling for Softies' holidays, which won BBC Radio 4's Enterprise Award in 1985 and were also chosen for the BBC television 1987 'holiday programme' series. For further information contact Susi Madron's Cycling Holidays Ltd, Lloyds House, 22 Lloyd Street, Manchester M2 5WA (061-834-6800).

Susi Madron's
CYCLING IN
FRANCE

Discover the Secret Heart of France

Susi Madron's

CYCLING IN FRANCE

Discover the Secret Heart of France

SUSI MADRON
AND
JOHN WALKER

GEORGE
PHILIP

Madron, Susi
   Susi Madron's cycling in France.
   1. Cycling—France—Handbooks, manuals, etc. 2. France—Handbooks, manuals, etc.
   I. Title   II. Walker, John
   914.4'04838'0247966   DC17
ISBN 0-540-01166-5

Text © John Walker 1988
Maps © George Philip 1988

First published by George Philip,
27A Floral Street, London WC2E 9DP

Maps by John Gilkes
Cartoons by David Till
Typeset by Tameside Filmsetting Limited
Lancashire
Printed in Great Britain by
Butler and Tanner Ltd, Frome and London

CONTENTS

INTRODUCTION

THIS BOOK HAS GROWN OUT OF my experience of running Susi Madron's Cycling for Softies, which offers tours in all the areas of France covered here. I have been cycling in France with my family for many years, and I started my holiday company simply because I wanted others to share the pleasures I had enjoyed. Riding a bicycle may be to you no more than a vague memory from youth but, as Bernard Shaw said, 'youth is wasted on the young'. A gentle cycling holiday is for mature, discerning romantics who like to linger over their pleasures, who want to relax and recharge their batteries so that they may regain some of the zest that the rest of the year has drained out of them.

Exploring France on a bike, away from the usual tourist haunts, is the best way I know to unwind, and to acquire a boundless capacity to enjoy simple pleasures: fresh air, sparkling streams, wayside flowers, a burst of butterflies by the roadside and delicious food and drink. As one of my regular holidaymakers wrote to me: 'So many of my favourite memories are of picnics high up in the hills, with stupendous views—and then an exhilarating free-wheel down to the valley afterwards. There is the sheer bliss of cycling for an hour or two without seeing any cars, and the awful torment of trying to decide which flavour of ice-cream to try next.'

Many of us have forgotten how liberating cycling can be, what ease and freedom it combines. It brings serendipity back into our lives, that wonderful capacity for encountering the unexpected—what H. G. Wells, who came from a generation who appreciated the bicycle, called 'the wheels of chance'. Cycling enables you to get closer not only to the countryside, but to the people who live in it. Many of those who go on our holidays return with tales of the kindness of those they meet along the way—of bags of cherries being proffered by children as they cycled past, or a farmer producing a glass of cider as they paused panting at the top of a hill.

One couple, returning to Châtillon in the Saône valley through the village of Saint-Etienne, feeling hot, sticky and rather weary, were overjoyed when a woman beckoned to them and invited them to swim in her pool and join her family in a cold drink. Another couple, looking appreciatively at the outside of an old mill, were shown over it by the owner, invited to eat their picnic in his garden under a sunshade and given a glass of kir.

The extraordinary kindness of the people in rural areas adds to the idyllic pleasure of pottering along the lazy country lanes past farms selling cheeses or small villages with shady restaurants. Picnics, too, become a pleasure, eating fresh croissants or rolls, delicious pastries and fruit sitting in a green field under the shade of a willow or poplar tree by a small stream.

Taking your time, peering over hedges and ancient walls, wandering off down little lanes and following enticing signs, gives you a totally new insight into France and the French. Memories of village fêtes with raucous · bands, magnificent fireworks and elaborate folk-costumes merge with those of excellent meals enjoyed over a couple of hours at the end of the day, of lovely manor houses and immaculate cottage gardens.

You need to move slowly to enjoy such pleasures. For that reason the stopping-places suggested here tend to be between 16 to 50 km (10 to 30 miles) apart, with day trips of around the same length. However, I have also included some suggestions for more exacting days from time to time. Many of the routes given here follow main roads, because that makes it easier for you when tracing them out on a map and planning where you want to go. But once you are on the spot, you will find many country lanes meander in the same direction and will provide you with cycling free from other traffic. Generally speaking, you should avoid the main N roads if there is an alternative route. At a gentle, pottering pace you will find that you can cover about 12 to 16 km (8 to 10 miles) in an hour so, with plenty of time to stop for leisurely picnics, and to explore the places you pass through, you can expect to spend around four hours in the saddle each day. The easiest cycling is in Mayenne-Sarthe, the Loire valley and the Venise Verte.

Remember that you will be taking your clothes with you, so travel as light as possible. I know that many dispense with everything that is not essential, including pyjamas! You need a bicycle with low ratio gears for easy touring, a set of panniers to hold your clothes, a handlebar bag or basket, a toolkit and puncture outfit for repairs, a pump and a water-bottle. A good map is essential. There are many available, but we recommend the 1:100,000 *Carte Topographique* series published by the Institut Géographique National. You should also carry a first-aid kit to deal with the occasional graze. Remember, too, that a loaded pannier on a bike alters its centre of gravity so that it can be a little disconcerting to ride at first. If you have not cycled for some time, it is best to avoid the hillier areas, as climbing and descending hills puts a great deal of strain on your wrists and arms when riding a laden bike. Some people prefer to go directly to the next hotel to dump their belongings before setting off to explore the area around.

If you do have a puncture or have to carry out other repairs, it is best to avoid putting the bits and pieces on the ground if you can. Nuts can be easily lost. You are unlikely to be as unlucky as the man whose pump was seized by a passing labrador, but it is amazing how parts disappear once they are no longer attached to the bicycle.

Even in the most northerly of our areas the weather is likely to be hot in summer. Pack a floppy hat and sunglasses and take plenty of suntan cream. It is also quite a good precaution to keep your arms covered as they can get very sunburnt. Remember too that detours can be tiring when the weather is hot. If you travel in a group, stay within sight of each other. It is easy for one person to take a wrong turning and get separated from the others, which can cause needless worry and distress.

How much will it cost? In a comfortable country hotel, usually providing an en suite bathroom and serving good regional food, you can expect to pay between 320 to 450 francs a night for two for dinner, bed and breakfast, but the very cheapest places may charge you as little as 140 francs (without bathroom). A couple might spend another 90 francs a day, although it is not difficult to get by on 20 to 40 francs each. Most of the hotels mentioned in this book are listed in the excellent annual publication *Logis et Auberges de France*, well worth consulting for family hotels throughout France.

If you have not touched a bike since your school days, then you may find it hard going in mid summer in a hilly district such as the Dordogne, where the sun can be fierce. Do plan your holiday to suit yourself. Instead of carrying your belongings around with you, you could settle on one town as a centre and make gentle outings each day into the surrounding area (when planning your routes remember you have to return from wherever you decide to visit). Occasionally, in some rural areas, you may find yourself chased down the road by dogs. More often than not, though, they will be chained and merely bark at you.

But whatever you decide, I hope the following pages will inspire you to saddle up and ride off into a French sunset. As someone once put it, 'Softies of the world unite. You have nothing to lose but your bicycle chains.'

CHAPTER ONE

MAYENNE AND SARTHE

THE DEPARTMENTS OF Mayenne and Sarthe are unknown territory to many visitors. Lying between Normandy to the north and the ever-popular Loire valley to the south, this enchanting countryside does not have the major attractions which draw tourists in their thousands, but it is ideal for the cyclist. This is the warm heart of rural France, a region of small towns, forgotten villages and tiny hamlets, of sparkling rivers and lakes and the remnants of former great forests. Tall poplars line the back roads like soldiers on parade and willows shade the little streams, marking their courses as they wind across country. Although there is nothing in Mayenne and Sarthe to match the grandest of the châteaux of the Loire, there are many fine buildings to be seen here. Grim fortresses bear witness to the endless local wars and almost continual invasions of the Middle Ages, and there are elegant country houses too, often just as fascinating as the more famous châteaux to the south. And even the smallest village has a crumbling medieval church.

You can swim in many of the lakes, several of which also offer sailing, canoeing and windsurfing. And there are opportunities for boating on the rivers too. Although the Paris–le Mans motorway cuts across the region, the roads are almost always quiet, so that you can enjoy the sights and sounds of the countryside: low stone-built farmhouses standing on the banks of streams, with chickens scratching nearby; horses working the fields; cows being milked by the roadside; clouds of butterflies fluttering over verges thickly studded with wild flowers. The villages, too, often feature stunning floral displays. Petunias and geraniums spill from window-boxes and twine around lamp-posts. Lettuces and cabbages grow between rows of asters and gladioli in the cottage gardens.

As elsewhere in France, in all these little communities you will find people ready and willing to offer help if it is needed. One cyclist, celebrating her 27th birthday, was travelling through

Saulges when a thunderstorm began. As the lightning flickered around and the torrential rain poured down, she decided to ask for refuge in a nearby farm. The farmer and his wife not only took her in, but insisted on providing her with a change of clothes. Then they offered her some cider and sat talking until the storm was over.

To cycle through this region is also to gain a strong sense of history. The Romans were here for five centuries and have left their mark in many places, such as the splendid fort at Jublains. Long before their great empire gathered strength, prehistoric peoples lived here, bequeathing clusters of standing stones and other neolithic monuments. Then there are the links with William the Conqueror's powerful state of Normandy just to the north, such as the ancient town of Mayenne which he besieged and largely destroyed. A century later, Mayenne and Sarthe lay on the borders of the territories of the Plantagenet kings, who ruled nearly the whole of western France as well as England (see p.48). In this century, many towns suffered terribly in the Second World War, while in recent decades there has been a steady drift of population from the countryside into the larger towns.

Being so close to Normandy, the regional cuisine has many links with that of the north-west corner of France. Except in the south, you will see apple orchards rather than vineyards and will be offered the local strong farmhouse cider to drink as an alternative to wine. Cider is also a principal ingredient in cooking. You can imagine a local Mrs Beeton beginning every recipe with 'First take some cider . . .'.

Fish from the many rivers also feature largely in the cuisine, and menus may include succulent trout cooked in cider served in a sauce made from cider and cream, or pike in cider butter sauce. Apples are often used to accompany dishes, and are made into mouth-watering tarts and desserts: who could resist apple charlotte with caramel mousse? Or you could end your meal

with a slice of the local cheese—the creamy Port Salut—washed
down with a glass of that fiery apple brandy known as Calvados.

The river Mayenne runs north to south, dividing the region
neatly into two. On its banks are the three main towns:
Mayenne itself in the north, the large, bustling city of Laval in
the centre, and Château-Gontier with its huge cattle market in
the south. You can travel directly to Mayenne and Sarthe by
train from Paris, stopping off either at Laval or at the busy market
town of Evron. None of these towns is so large as to be
intimidating. Laval, the largest, has a population of around
50,000, three or four times bigger than Mayenne and Château-
Gontier.

Everywhere else you visit is likely to be home to fewer than a
thousand people and many villages, like the tiny Saint-Erblon or
Bannes, have only a hundred or so inhabitants. For the most part,
cycling is easy here. Many of the most interesting towns and
villages straddle rivers or streams and you will find yourself
following the valleys rather than climbing hills. Climatically,
north-west France is much closer to England than it is to
Provence, but it can still get very hot in the summer and you will
need a sunhat and suntan oil. It can also be very humid, with
sudden thunderstorms bringing torrential downpours, but most
rain falls in the autumn and winter. Spring is often the nicest
season, with frosty mornings and bright days. Like Britain, the
climate is rarely extreme, and snow is uncommon. Average
temperatures range from around 24°C at the height of summer
to 4°C in the January cold.

You could cycle without difficulty down the length of the
region from Mayenne to Château-Gontier (a distance of some
60 km), making detours on the way to visit the many places of
interest. A good route for those short of time would take you
from Mayenne to Jublains, with its Gallo-Roman remains, and
from there down the D7 to Evron, with its magnificent basilica of

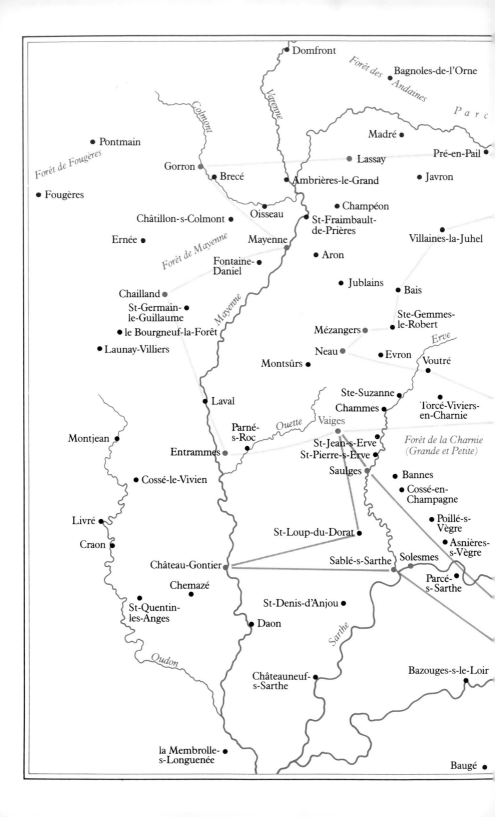

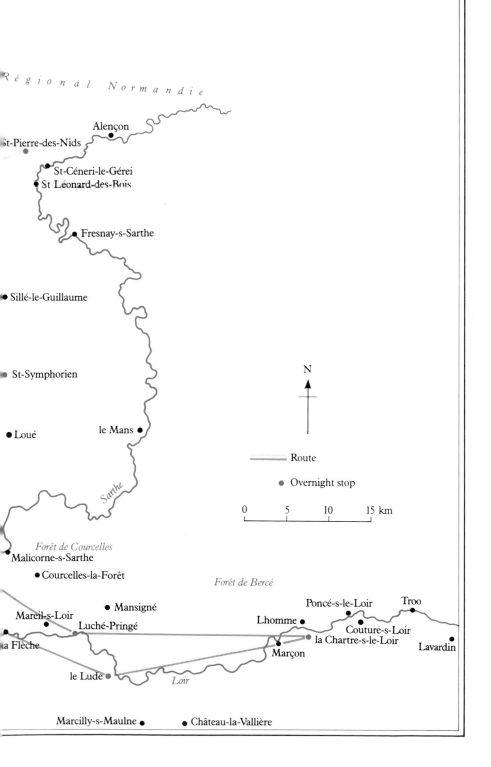

Notre-Dame, a total distance of 24 km. You could stop for rest and refreshment at Evron before continuing on along the same road to the fortified town of Sainte-Suzanne, where you branch off on to the D125 to Vaiges. This leg adds another 19 km, making a total of 43 for the day. You could spend the night at Vaiges and then cycle for 10 km through Saint-Pierre-sur-Erve and Saulges, which is worth a stop, partly to see the prehistoric caves but especially for food. The final lap would take you from Saulges through Ballée, le Buret, Saint-Charles-la-Forêt and Ruille-Froid-Fonds to Château-Gontier, another 35 km further.

On such a jaunt, you would have been able to see archaeological sites and formidable châteaux, cycling along gentle rivers and through villages that seem to have hardly changed since the Middle Ages. And you would have eaten and drunk well. It is even more enjoyable to spend a week or a fortnight exploring the area more thoroughly.

By staying in a village such as Vaiges, which is near the centre of the region, you could make a number of fascinating excursions into the countryside around. For instance, covering 40 km a day, you could visit Sainte-Suzanne, Evron and Mézangers with its marvellous château on one day, and travel on to Saint-Pierre-sur-Erve, Saulges, Chémeré-le-Roi and Saint-Denis-du-Maine, where you can swim or water-ski on the lake, on another.

In a week or ten days based in Vaiges a good tour of the lush green countryside to the south would involve overnight stops at Château-Gontier, Sablé or Solesmes, le Lude, la Chartre, Luché-Pringé and Saulges. In a fortnight you could travel north to the apple-growing areas on the edge of Normandy and visit Entrammes, Chailland, Mayenne, Gorron, Lassay, Saint-Pierre, Mézangers, Neau and Saint-Symphorien before returning to Vaiges.

Vaiges itself is 23 km east of Laval, on the N157 to le Mans, and just over a kilometre from the no. 2 exit on the Paris—

le Mans–Rennes motorway. A village of some 900 inhabitants, where everybody not only knows everyone else but seems to be related to them in a vast network of cousins, Vaiges has few shops, though it manages to support two ironmongers and two bakers, where you can buy bread still warm from the ovens in the mornings. There is also a grocer, and the butcher has expanded by opening a supermarket. The church was devastated by fire some years ago, when a lorry crashed into it, but this proved a blessing in disguise when a fresco was discovered during the renovations. Monsieur le Curé is proud of his church and is delighted to show people round. Ask at the *mairie* (French mayors still retain a central place in their communities) to see the museum with its local history collection. The Hôtel du Commerce, which has been run by the Oger family for more than a hundred years, is recommended here.

North-east of Vaiges, 12 km away on the D125, is the fortified medieval town of Sainte-Suzanne, standing on a hilltop above the surrounding wooded countryside, with the river Erve running at its foot. The hill is rocky and precipitous, and has proved a deterrent to many would-be conquerors over the centuries. William the Conqueror, plagued by unrest and rebellion on the borders of Normandy in the years after his triumph in England, spent four years in the 1080s unsuccessfully besieging it. Then it was occupied by the English in the Hundred Years War. Much of the violent history of this ancient place is recorded in the little museum, open in the afternoon during the summer months. You can recover your strength in the Restaurant Relais du Fouquet, or in the small village of Chammes on the way back, where the delightful Mme Loison runs an old-fashioned café which you will recognize by the flowers on the window-sill.

Château-Gontier is 40 km to the south-west. Take the D24 south to Saint-Loup-du-Dorat, turning left on to the D21 and then immediately right on to the D212. After about 2 km you turn right again, on to the D28. The best day to visit this bustling little town is 14 July, when a stunning firework display explodes over the river. For the locals, this is an important agricultural centre, with a sheep and cattle market every Thursday and the largest calf market in Europe. The old town is full of winding narrow streets and 300-year-old houses, although much of it was severely battered during the long religious wars of the 1500s. Many old buildings survive nevertheless, including the 11th-century church of Saint-Jean-Baptiste, once attached to the château of Foulques Nerra, Count of Anjou. The beautiful crypt has a triple nave with red sandstone pillars. The Chapelle de Geneteil, which dates from the 12th century, is also worth a visit. There is a town festival from 15 August to the end of the month. On the road to Angers out of the old town is the delightful Hôtel le Parc. This little château is still surrounded by its park, and has the added attraction of a swimming-pool (open from July) and a tennis court. You can eat at the Hôtel la Brasserie a few hundred metres away.

On a day trip from Château-Gontier you could sample some more good food at the Auberge du Roy René in Saint-Denis-d'Anjou, 20 km to the east along the D105 and D27. This old village has a splendid barn-like market, built in 1509, with a great, steep, tiled roof raised on wooden pillars. Or visit Craon, on the banks of the river Oudon, 19 km west of Château-Gontier on the D22. This small town is best known for its racecourse, pleasingly laid out in a natural hollow surrounded by small hillocks. Horse-racing addicts should be sure to be here in September, when the population of the town doubles in size for five race meetings, culminating in a steeplechase and a trotting race held on the third Sunday in the month. Those more culturally inclined may like to visit the Château de Craon, built in a classical 18th-century style and with an interior to match the magnificent exterior. Unfortunately, although the grounds are open during July and August, you have to write in advance for permission to see inside the building.

Château enthusiasts should return to Château-Gontier through Saint-Quentin-les-Anges, 10 km from Craon on the D25, to see the Château de Mortier-Crolle. Built just before 1500, this striking building looms over a wide moat, looking more Italian than French. Then go north-east through Chemazé, where the white stone Château de Saint-Ouen is a masterpiece of renaissance architecture.

You can probably see the greatest concentration of châteaux in the area by going south on the D162 to Angers, a town dealt with more fully in the chapter on the châteaux of the Loire (see p.55). Turn left on to the D611 some 6 km out of Château-Gontier and a short ride brings you to the brick-built formality of the Château de Magnanne, which has an interesting interior. Returning to the D162 you pass the part medieval, part renaissance Château du Percher on the left after 5 km or so and then, just east of the highway in a beautiful lakeside setting, the Château du Bois-Mauboucher, which dates in part from the 1400s. At le Lion d'Angers is the 18th-century Château de l'Isle Briand, on an island between the Mayenne and the Oudun, but of greater interest is the Château du Plessis-Macé some 10 km further on—turn right on to the D105 at la Membrolle-sur-Longuenée. At least three French kings stayed in this moated building dating from the 12th century when on hunting expeditions, including Louis XI.

Whatever else you see you should not miss the Château du Plessis-Bourré, 16 km north-east across the Mayenne, or 35 km from Château-Gontier down the D22, D859 and D108 (a charming road following the Sarthe). Open from April to September, the château is a white-walled fortress dating from the 1460s. It was built by Jean Bourré, Treasurer to Louis XI and

Charles VIII, with a sumptuousness unusual in the 15th century. But there is no trace of comfort in the exterior. The arched bridge crossing the broad moat ends in a narrow drawbridge and a fortified gateway. Pepperpot towers rise from the massive walls. Today the interior is full of fine 18th-century furniture and the first-floor guardroom still has a 15th-century painted ceiling depicting fables and proverbs. If you return to Château-Gontier through Daon you could make a little detour to the right on the D213 to the Manoir d'Escoublère, a moated, fortified manor house with four round towers, dating from the 1470s.

The next stop is at Sablé-sur-Sarthe or Solesmes, only 7 km apart. Sablé-sur-Sarthe is a small town of some 12,000 inhabitants, 30 km to the east of Château-Gontier along the D28 and D306. Its large château, built in the early 18th century by a nephew of Colbert, overlooks the river. The old-fashioned Hôtel Saint Martin off the Rue St Martin in the old part of town is entered through a delightful little courtyard covered in wisteria and creepers. Market days are Monday and Friday.

At Solesmes we stay in the Grand Hôtel, which is a surprise. Outside it looks medieval, but inside there is a modern extension to provide extra dining facilities and bedrooms. M. Bertrand Jaquet, the proprietor, speaks perfect English and runs an excellent restaurant. You can fish in the river Sarthe and may be able to take a boat out. There are market days on Monday and Friday and a guitar festival during August.

But the great attraction here is Solesmes' lofty St Peter's abbey, which has the appearance of a gothic château. This monastery, head of the Benedictine Order in France, is best seen from across the river or from the bridge. The abbey itself was built in 1896 with a new wing being added as recently as 1956, although most of the church dates from the 15th century and the romanesque arches of the nave are 400 years older. The monks have gained a worldwide reputation for their singing of the ancient Gregorian chant and have made records that help pay for the abbey's upkeep. You can hear their sonorous and uplifting voices every morning and evening at services in the church, the only times when visitors are allowed in the abbey. Singing by the women's choir at the neighbouring church of Saint-Cecilia has also been much praised.

There are two small towns nearby that are worth a ride. North-east along the D22 is the pretty Asnières-sur-Vègre, with its old houses, a 12th-century bridge and an 11th-century church containing some interesting murals. Some 2 km further on you can see the 16th-century Château de Verdelles, and there is an ancient bridge of pointed arches over the river at Poillé-sur-Vègre. (To visit the château, call at the nearby farm.) Parcé-sur-Sarthe on a bend in the river 10 km east of Solesmes on the D309 is equally pretty. If you turn right on to the D8 here, you will come to Malicorne-sur-Sarthe after about 20 km, where there is a pottery museum and workshop open every afternoon from Easter to September.

On the way to the elegant town of le Lude, 46 km south of Sablé-sur-Sarthe on the D306, pause for refreshment in la Flèche. The philosopher Descartes and many of France's greatest generals once studied at the famous military college here. Just outside the town is the Zoo du Tertre Rouge, run by the naturalist Jacques Bouillant, which is more a village for animals than a conventional zoo. Some 800 creatures ranging from lions and tigers to elephants, llamas and kangaroos are kept in the extensive grounds, which also include a bird park.

From here you could make a short detour west for 7 km on the N23 to Bazouges-sur-le-Loir, where there is another breath-taking little château, glowing golden-brown in the sun on a river bank. You can visit it from Easter to September. The town's partly 12th-century church is also of interest, containing some painted wooden vaults dating from the 1400s.

Le Lude itself is dominated by its magnificent fortress of a château with a renaissance façade moulded on to the massive defences of the original building. The interior is beautifully furnished and the room Henry IV (1553–1610) slept in can still be seen as it was when he used it. The château gardens are open in the morning, but the interior can only be seen in the afternoon. Le Lude is also famous for its *son-et-lumière*, the finest in France and the most elaborate you are ever likely to see, which is held below the château on Friday and Saturday evenings in summer. More than 300 actors are involved in retelling 500 years of the château's history.

The Hôtel du Maine at le Lude is a small building by the level-crossing of the now defunct railway line. We always like staying here because you can sit in the garden at the back and enjoy a pre-dinner cocktail in the warmth of the evening, or even snooze in the afternoon sun. Le Lude is also the northernmost point of the vineyards that produce the wines of the Loire, and you can sample the dry white or sparkling wines of Vouvray here. There is fishing and boating on the river and market day is Thursday.

To the north, 37 km along the D307, is le Mans, the most famous town in Sarthe and the capital of the region. It has plenty to recommend it even for those not interested in its 24-hour motor race or its museum of vintage cars and motorcycles. At the centre of the old quarter of the town is the magnificent Saint-Julien's cathedral, named after the saint who preached there in the 4th century. Building began in the 11th century and was completed in the 15th, so that it encompasses both the romanesque and the gothic styles. The pleasure-loving poet and satirist Paul Scarron (1610–60) was an honorary canon at the cathedral, and his widow, the somewhat frigid and religious Madame de Maintenon, moved on to become governess to Louis XIV's bastard children and then secretly married the king in 1688.

The cathedral is full of interest, not least because it contains the 13th-century marble tomb of Queen Berengaria, wife of Richard the Lionheart. The daughter of the King of Navarre, she founded the Cistercian abbey at Epau 4 km west of le Mans a year before her death in 1230. If you can, visit the abbey at night, when the buildings are floodlit. Or you can walk and picnic in the woods round about. Queen Berengaria's house still stands in the old city of le Mans, in a street of medieval houses. You can also see traces of the city wall built by the Romans.

A shorter day trip from le Lude would be to take the D959 through wooded country to Château-la-Vallière, which stands on the edge of a vast lake, the Etang du Val Joyeux. A detour west along the D766 and then right on to the D66 on the return journey would enable you to see the moated château at Marcilly-sur-Maulne, which is open two days a week. Continuing north from the village on back roads brings you back to the D959 some 4 km from le Lude.

To the south-west of le Lude, 25 km along the D305 and D817, is the old town of Baugé. This is also a pleasant ride, through farmland and forest. The former château, now the town hall, dates from the 1430s, and you can also visit the Hôpital Saint-Joseph, where a fine collection of old faïence pots is displayed in the panelled pharmacy. Of greater interest is a cross with two arms in the Chapel of the Incurables. Brought from Constantinople by returning Crusaders in the 13th century and now ornamented with gold and precious stones, it is said to have been made from pieces of the True Cross. This is the original of the celebrated Cross of Lorraine, which became the symbol of the Free French during the Second World War.

One of the delights of this area is the geraniums that adorn so many of the buildings, including the Hôtel de France in a small square in the centre of the next stop: la Chartre-sur-le-Loir. This small country town surrounded by vineyards is some 37 km east of le Lude along the D305. You can swim in the river Loir here or in the lake at Marçon some 7 km downstream, which is used for water-sports, or in the local pool. Market day is on Thursday.

The surrounding countryside is some of the most attractive and peaceful we have found and is studded with interesting churches and châteaux, such as the one at Poncé-sur-le-Loir, 9 km east of the D305, which stands at the foot of a cliff. The château grounds include an incredible maze and what is said to be one of the finest dovecotes in France. If you go inside the château, do look up at the magnificent ceiling as you climb the renaissance staircase. The château is open from March to early November, although there is no access for two hours at lunchtime and on Sunday mornings. If you are unlucky enough to find it closed, visit the arts and crafts centre nearby or look at the murals in the ancient church. Executed in 1180, these include a battle between Christians and Saracens, presumably a reference to the Crusades.

Continue for another 2 km along the D305 and then turn right to Couture-sur-Loir, where the greatest French poet of his time, Pierre de Ronsard, was born in 1524 in the Manoir de la Possonnière. If you return to the D305 and continue east you come to the ancient hilltop town of Troo, with its remarkable troglodyte dwellings carved out of the chalk cliffs. The medieval Maladerie-Sainte-Catherine here, a hospital for lepers and the diseased, recalls the time when the town was a stopping-point for pilgrims on their way to Tours. Another 7 km east is the ruined castle at Lavardin, which the English besieged without success in the 1180s.

To the north of la Chartre are the lovely woods of the Forêt de Bercé, where you could spend a day happily wandering beneath ancient oak trees, chestnuts and pines. The road there takes you through Lhomme, where you can see the dolmen du Pierre Maupertuis.

La Chartre is the easternmost point of this tour and the next stopover, Luché-Pringé, is 46 km west. The Auberge du Port des Roches, 3 km from the centre of the village on the D214 towards le Lude, is smothered in flowers and has the Loir flowing past its front door. To the north-west, 6 km along the D13, is the pretty village of Mareil-sur-Loir, a delightful short ride through open country. Halfway there you will pass the Château of Gallerande, dating from the 1400s. Cycle north-east on the same road for 4 km and you come to the fortified Manoir de Venevelles. If the weather is hot, continue on for another 6 km and you can swim in the lake at Mansigné. North of Luché-Pringé is the Forêt de Courcelles, with wooded areas interspersed with more open stretches of country covered in wild broom. To get a taste of both, ride north-west along the D54 to the pretty village of Courcelles-la-Forêt and then take the D8 to Malicorne-sur-Sarthe, with its pottery works and museum. This is a round trip of about 40 km.

From Luché-Pringé go north to Saulges, a village in the valley of the river Erve which is but a very short ride from Vaiges. Take the D306 through la Flèche and Sablé-sur-Sarthe and then turn right on to the D24 and D235, a journey of 48 km. Although Saulges is small, it has two interesting churches, one dating from the 17th century. We like to stay at l'Ermitage in the centre of the village. This is an excellent hotel and restaurant, although the saintly hermit who came to live nearby some 1300 years ago would probably not have approved of the good food it provides, such as *aiguillette de canard au vinaigre de framboise*, thin slices of duck served with a dressing made with raspberry vinegar.

The hermit, St Cenere, seems to have been attracted by the river, and it is easy to understand how the broad, quiet stretch of water here aided his contemplative life. He died by the Erve in 680, and is commemorated in a shrine behind an old mill by the river to the west of the village. This can be visited, although it is approached by a steep and sometimes slippery stepped path. The 7th-century church of Saint-Pierre nearby has recently been restored. Saulges holds a village festival on the second Sunday in August and a fishing competition in the middle of the month.

Follow the river north through its pretty valley for 3 km along the D235 and you arrive at the tiny village of Saint-Pierre-sur-Erve, with a charming church dating from the 12th century. On the way, you cross over an arched bridge with ivy climbing up the sides that was built more than 700 years ago. Between Saint-Pierre and Saulges are the Grotte de Rochefort and the Grotte à Margot, cool and sometimes damp caves which were once the home of prehistoric man. Unfortunately, the most interesting cavern, which contains some superb wall-paintings of bison and mammoth, has been closed because it was being attacked by fungus. At one time you could explore the caves on your own, but this was stopped when two ladies went in and never came out again. These days, there is a guide to show you the fantastic formations of stalactites and stalagmites and the little underground lake.

There are several other villages in the area worth a look, such as Saint-Jean-sur-Erve, just to the north of Saint-Pierre, which has existed since the 1000s and has interesting old houses. Another good reason for calling in here is that it is famous locally for its succulent brioches. You could make a round trip by going on to Bannes along the D58 and D7. Fewer than 200 people live in the village now, but its ancient moated manor house survives and there are some 14th-century murals in the tiny 12th-century church. Cossé-en-Champagne a little further south also boasts a 12th-century church and a medieval manor. Vaiges is so close to Saulges, just 11 km north, that you could easily see all these villages on the final leg of the tour.

On the northern exploration of the area, the first stop is Entrammes, 33 km to the west of Vaiges if you go straight down the main road to Laval and then south. A much nicer and more direct route is to cycle across country by small, winding roads, along the D152 and D233. Entrammes is famous as the home of the creamy Port Salut cheese which was created by monks at the Benedictine abbey here, although it is now produced at a new factory next to the monastery. The Hôtel le Lion d'Or in the centre of the village has a well-deserved reputation for delicious meals, with a menu featuring *magret de canard au cidre*, breast of duck cooked in cider, and a dish that combines chicken and the local cheese, *poulet au fromage de l'abbaye*. The village festival is held on the last weekend in August.

Entrammes lies between Laval to the north and Château-Gontier to the south. The valley of the Mayenne between these two towns is a delight of water and woods and ancient hamlets, many of them now with a much reduced population. Most of these tiny places have an interesting church that is likely to have been built around the 15th century, although it will probably have been much restored in the 19th. Parné-sur-Roc, 6 km east of Entrammes on the D103, is typical of the valley. A village full of flowers by the river Ouette, its priory was founded in 1094 and parts of the church date from the 12th century.

Laval, the capital of Mayenne, straddles the river of the same name 10 km to the north of Entrammes. The town is grouped around the grim château of the counts of Laval, built on the foundations of an even earlier fortress, with a massive keep dating from the 12th century. Nearby a medieval bridge crosses the river, one of only two linking the banks. Several remarkable individuals were born in Laval, including the primitive painter Henri 'Le Douanier' Rousseau, and Alfred Jarry, the novelist and playwright who scandalized Paris in the 1890s with *Ubu Roi*, his exuberant farce on bourgeois respectability. Rousseau, who died in 1910, is buried here. There is a splendid view of the town and its medieval château from the Jardin de la Perrine where he lies.

The château contains a museum of primitive painting and, although Rousseau's masterpieces are to be found elsewhere, it does display one of his works.

Laval is a delightful town to wander through and there are many buildings of interest. In 1554 Jacques Marest, one of the richest merchants of this region, built a house in the classical style, the Maison du Grand Veneur, that still stands as evidence of his wealth and taste. Then there is the Château de Bel-Air, a miniature Versailles. Do visit the church of Notre-Dame-d'Avénières beyond the Jardin de la Perrine, not only because it is a magnificent building but also because it is in such a beautiful position. It is best seen from the far bank of the Mayenne, with the church reflected in the water. From across the river the building forms a series of triangular shapes which rise one above the other and culminate in its high spire. Inside, there is a statue of Christ on tiptoe, about to ascend into heaven.

Halfway between Laval and the small and delightful market town of Craon to the south on the N171 (see p.24) is Cossé-le-Vivien, which it is worth visiting to see the Musée Robert Tatin, with its garden full of unusual sculpture that combines the naïve and the surrealistic. The river Oudon, a tributary of the Mayenne, adds its charms to the countryside here and there are several small and interesting villages along its banks. Return to Laval along the D124 past the romantic ruins of the moated 15th-century château of Montjean. Or you could go on past Cossé to see the remains of Roman goldmines at Livré, on the D286 to the right. This village also has the 15th-century Château de l'Eperonnière and a church of the same period. Another good outing from Entrammes is to visit the ruins of the huge and austere Clermont Abbey, founded by St Bernard in the 11th century. It is set amid lovely woods to the west of Laval.

Chailland, the next stopover, is 35 km north. It is a small, quiet village, on the edge of the Forêt de Mayenne which stretches away to the north-east. At the tiny, simple Hôtel des Voyageurs M. Chauvois is an excellent chef who conjures up memorable meals. Walk to the Rochers de la Vierge et du Calvaire above the village and you will be rewarded by a splendid view, as well as working up a good appetite. Guarding the valley, 4 km south-east of Chailland on the D165, is the 14th-century Château du Mesnil at Saint-Germain-le-Guillaume. A photogenic old watermill stands nearby.

Some 11 km south-west of Chailland on the D31 and D123 is le Bourgneuf-la-Forêt, where you could treat yourself to lunch at the Hôtel Vieille Auberge. This delightful rural hostelry was once a coaching inn and retains that atmosphere, with its heavy oak beams and magnificent fireplace in the reception area. It is worth going on a few kilometres to see the picturesque hamlet of Launay-Villiers, which has a 19th-century château (not open) and the remains of a castle built in the 14th century. There is also a charming waterfall on the stream here and an old mill by the water's edge.

North of Chailland, 14 km away on the D31, is Ernée, set in another delightful river valley. You can fish and swim in the river here, and the town has a little museum of prehistoric and Roman finds from the area. You could visit Ernée on the way to Mayenne, the next stop, which lies directly east. Or you could wander to Mayenne across country, along back roads from Chailland. Set on the river of the same name, Mayenne is a charming town with pleasant shops that was once the capital of the region—a title it has lost to Laval. It has suffered much over the centuries, from William the Conqueror's burning of the town in 1064 to the destruction of many buildings during the Second World War. There is a good view of the town and the river from the remains of the once formidable 11th-century château, with its single round tower. We like to stay in the Grand Hôtel here, set close by the river. Its attractions include indoor and outdoor swimming-pools, and a menu featuring such specialities as duck in cider. Markets are held in Mayenne on Monday and Saturday and there is a town festival during the third week in July.

Any exploration of the countryside around should take you to Jublains, where there are extensive remains of the Roman occupation of the area, including a temple, a theatre and fortifications. Many of the walls look as sturdy as when they were built, with layers of stone sandwiched between rows of brick. The site is only 10 km east along the D35 to Aron and then right on to the D7. On the way you pass the large Etang de Beaucoudray on the left.

South-west of Mayenne, 9 km away on the wooded D104, Fontaine-Daniel is an unusual and picturesque village with a splendid tea-shop. Fontaine was built for the weavers of the local mill, an operation that now produces cloth and curtain material in 400 colours. Another interesting village is Champéon, 11 km north-east of Mayenne, just off the D34 between it and the delightful Lassay. There is an extraordinary dovecote here at the Château de Fresne. Built in the 1530s, it stands on eight pillared legs in the middle of an island in a small lake, looking for all the world like a small house going for a paddle. You can paddle, swim or indulge in water-sports at Ambrières-le-Grand only a few kilometres across country from Champéon. This is a pleasant old town which has traces of prehistoric and Roman occupation. It is built at the confluence of the Varenne and Mayenne in another of the beautiful valleys that are characteristic of the region. Two detours are worth making on the way back to Mayenne. The first is to Saint-Fraimbault-de-Prières, another centre for water-sports, which is just 3 km east of the D23. The other is to Oisseau, directly across country on the other side of the D23. Another ancient village (it was first mentioned in 832), Oisseau has associations with Joan of Arc and is set in the beautiful valley of the river Colmont.

Gorron, the next stopping-place, is 27 km north-west of Mayenne, delightfully situated on a little lake in the valley of the Colmont. At one time its position was of strategic importance and William the Conqueror laid siege to Gorron two years before he invaded England. There are old houses in the town and you can see prehistoric remains nearby. Stay in the Hôtel de Bretagne on the lake, which is run by two generations of the Louvigne family (the son speaks excellent English). Market day is on Wednesdays. On the way to Gorron you will pass through Châtillon-sur-Colmont, with its prehistoric standing stones, 16th-century manor house, and a village festival on the last Sunday in June. This sleepy village in its river valley typifies France at its most rural and peaceful. Just before Gorron there is a 15th-century gothic church at Brecé. If you decide to stop here, ask to see the cool, massively arched vaults.

Pilgrims have visited Pontmain, 24 km west of Gorron, in increasing numbers following a vision of the Virgin Mary there in 1871. Some of the ecclesiastical buildings in the town are medieval, but the most notable is the 19th-century neo-gothic basilica of Notre-Dame, built to commemorate the event. It has twin spires, and a carillon of 32 bells. To get to Pontmain, turn right off the D33 at la Tannière and then left on to the D290 at Saint-Mars-sur-la-Futaie, a little village with a medieval church.

South-west of Pontmain, 15 km down the D19 and D177, is the fortified town of Fougères, set on a promontory above a bend of the river Nancon and for centuries in a key position on the border between Brittany and Normandy. There is a magnificent medieval castle here with massive, high walls studded with 13 towers. The keep was destroyed in the 1100s, but you can still see the outline of its foundations. The walls enclose a huge area, best appreciated from the top of the 14th-century tower known as la Mélusine. The church of Saint-Sulpice just south of the castle dates from the 15th century and contains some good 18th-century wood carvings. If you ride to Fougères from Pontmain, you come through the remnants of the Forêt de Fougères, where there are megalithic remains, including dolmens. Gorron is 32 km east along the D806 and D33.

The next stop is the charming medieval town of Lassay, 25 km east of Gorron along the D33. The tiny Auberge du Lassay in the main square is run by M. and Mme Bourgeois, two Parisians who came here on holiday and never went home. Their specialities include veal chop *flambée aux Calvados* and veal escalope cooked in cider.

On summer weekends an elaborate *son-et-lumière* takes place against the backdrop of the château. It is held on Tuesdays, Fridays and Saturdays during June, and on Fridays and Saturdays during July and August. The château was rebuilt in 1547 to replace an earlier fortress destroyed by the English during the Hundred Years War. It is just how you would expect a fortress to look, with high walls some 2 metres thick punctuated by eight even higher massive round towers. A few tiny slits let in a little light and provided vantage points for bowmen. The lower windows of the towers overlook the walls, so that defenders could shoot anyone trying to scale them, but there is a panoramic view over the surrounding countryside from the ones just under the conical roofs. The castle is entered across a fearsome drawbridge, flanked by two towers. The château is closed on Mondays. There is a village festival at the end of July and market day is on Wednesday.

You can get a flavour of how life used to be at the ancient village of Madré 11 km north-east of Lassay along the D34 and D214. The evocative agricultural museum here is a working farm that uses old horse-drawn methods, and sometimes offers carriage rides to visitors.

The road north, the D34, also leads after 16 km to the Normandy spa town of Bagnoles-de-l'Orne, a fashionable centre for the treatment of various ailments based on the hot springs here. The position of the town is exceptionally attractive. Set on a lake on the edge of the vast Normandy-Maine Regional Park, it is surrounded by the fir woods of the Forêt des Andaines. At the western end of the forest is the fortified town of Domfront, which has a ruined castle and an 11th-century church where Thomas Becket celebrated mass. It is 18 km from Lassay along the D117 and D22.

To the east of Lassay, where the river Sarthe forms the border with Mayenne, is the pretty, lively village of Saint-Pierre-des-Nids. Make your way across country to Pré-en-Pail, turning right on to the D144 for the final stretch, a total distance of 37 km. As you go east the countryside becomes gradually hillier and you pass the highest point in the region, the Mont des Avaloirs, just outside Pré-en-Pail along the D144. If you feel like taking time out of the saddle, there is a marvellous panoramic view of the surrounding countryside from the top, over 410 metres above sea-level. Saint-Pierre's Hôtel du Dauphin at the end of the ride is always welcoming. It is run by the extremely affable M. Etienne, President of the hôteliers of Mayenne, whose menu features such regional dishes as *poulet pomme d'abeille, foie gras chaud aux deux pommes* and *sorbet aux Calvados*.

You can also eat well in the splendid restaurants of Alençon, the main town of the region 15 km east on the D121 and D1. Once famous for lace-making, Alençon was also the birthplace in 1873 of St Thérèse of Lisieux, who entered a Carmelite convent at the age of 15 and died there nine years later. Despite her relatively short experience of the religious life, her account of her simple faith found a wide audience and led to her canonization in the 1920s. The gothic church of Notre-Dame was built in the 1400s, around the same time as the town's fortress, which was once the seat of the dukes of Alençon and is now a prison. Deer and wild boar roam in the Forêt d'Écouves 5 km to the north.

Saint-Cenéri-le-Gérei, some 4 km south-east of Saint-Pierre on the D144, has some interesting frescoes in its 12th-century church. This village lies on the edge of a charming, hilly district known as the Alps Mancelles, which is well worth exploring. Go south from Saint-Céneri for a further 5 km along the D146 to Saint-Léonard-des-Bois, an engaging village by the Sarthe. Continue along the winding road and then follow the D112 and D15 to Fresnay-sur-Sarthe, an old town set on a hill above the river with the remains of a castle.

You could visit these villages on the way to the next stopover, the very attractive village of Mézangers, 40 km south-west of Saint-Pierre. The more direct route is by the D121 to Villaines-la-Juhel, and then south on the D20 through Bais to Sainte-Gemmes-le-Robert, turning right on to the D517 for the final stretch. At the junction with the D7, turn right again for the Relais du Gue de Selle, about 1 km from the village on the road to Jublains. An old farmhouse converted into a smart hotel, the Relais overlooks a lake which is used for water-sports. Mézangers has a village festival on the last Sunday in July. The ground rises to the north, culminating in the nearby Butte de Montaigu (along the D7 and D236) and Mont Rochard (along the D20), both of which are worth climbing for the gorgeous views of the surrounding area.

Mézangers also has the attraction of the Château du Rocher just to the west. With its towers and high grey roofs reflected in the waters of a lake, this beautiful renaissance building has a dreamlike quality. Although the interior is not open, you can walk in the grounds and marvel at its perfection. You could also retrace your steps to Bais to see the Château de Montesson, dating from the late 16th century. A squat, powerful building, it has a tower with a curious bulbous roof that looks like an up-ended, old-fashioned motorhorn. It, too, is not open to the public, and neither is the extremely attractive moated Château de

Foulletorte, 15 km east of Mézangers along the D32 and D143 from Evron. Built of granite it stands on the edge of a wide expanse of water, surrounded by gentle wooded hills.

Evron owes its existence to a pilgrim who was returning from the Holy Land in the 600s with a relic containing some of the Virgin Mary's milk. He hung it on a thornbush for the night while he slept and, by next morning, the bush had grown so much that the relic was out of his reach. He tried to cut the bush down, but his hatchet stuck in its trunk. The Bishop of le Mans was summoned and the thornbush shrank to its normal size when he knelt before the relic. A church was founded on the spot and the basilica of Notre-Dame now on the site has few equals in this region. The tower dates from the 11th century, although the nave, transept and choir were built in the 14th century and the high altar some 400 years later. The fine statue of the Virgin in the chapel of Notre-Dame, carved of wood inlaid with silver and enamel, is known as Our Lady of the Thorn after the legend. Evron's market day is Thursday, and a festival is held here during the first week in September.

Some 10 km east of Evron is Voutré, with its excellent restaurant, La Croix Verte—try the calf's kidneys *aux Calvados*. At the next halt, in the village of Neau only a few kilometres from Mézangers, is another hotel and restaurant of the same name, De la Croix Verte, where the food is also superb. You can eat such regional dishes as pike in a white butter sauce, flavoured with wine and shallots (a recipe that was created at Nantes on the Loire not far away), and a delicious tart made from the local apples.

Neau is another sleepy country village, with a church dating from the 9th century, but with many later additions. Market day is on Thursday. To the west is the larger village of Montsûrs, where you can see the ruins of a château that was burned by the English in 1430. Market day here is on Tuesday.

The last stop before the return to Vaiges is the tiny village of Saint-Symphorien, set amidst beautiful woods. Go east along the D32 and D234 to Voutré, and then south-east along the D146, D9 and D28. The proprietor of the Relais de la Charnie will arrange horse-riding for those who would like it.

There is plenty of good eating to be found in this area. Loué 12 km to the south has a fine restaurant and there is also excellent cooking at Torcé-Viviers, 14 kilometres to the west, where the small L'Orée de la Charnie is run by M. Reant, who trained at Vaiges' Hôtel du Commerce. The menu here features delicious snails and pike *au beurre blanc*. The surrounding woods of the Forêt-de-la-Charnie provide a feast for the eye and you can swim in large tree-lined lakes 15 km to the north of Saint-Symphorien near the town of Sillé-le-Guillaume. From Saint-Symphorien, it is 35 km back to Vaiges.

Travel south to Angers and you come to the Loire valley, an area that also has secret places unknown to the many tourists who see no more than its famous châteaux.

CHAPTER TWO

CHÂTEAUX OF THE LOIRE

THE LOIRE VALLEY is known worldwide for its magnificent châteaux, buildings that range from medieval fortresses to sumptuous palaces. Unfortunately this means that it is also a tourist trap. It often seems that you pays your money and . . . you pays your money. Yet, despite the Loire's popularity, it also contains beautiful countryside that is almost unknown and unvisited by the mass of tourists.

The little twisting lanes that run through the serene landscape and friendly villages of this region of France are ideal for those who like gentle, tranquil cycling. You can wander for hours along quiet valleys, where lovely rivers such as the Thouet, Cher, Vienne and Indre flow by magnificent and little known châteaux. Away from the tourist traps there are secret beauty spots and countryside that is as attractive as it is little visited.

Vineyards and fields of sunflowers and wheat stretch to the horizon, with only the occasional stand of poplar trees breaking up the smooth, flat landscape. History oozes from the warm, cream stone of the elegant houses, from the ancient walls still surrounding many towns and villages, and from the old farm buildings. Often houses are centred round small well-kept courtyards festooned with flowers.

The valley of the Loire also has other, less obvious attractions. If the châteaux are monuments to a rich and sometimes bloody past, the land itself is famous for more prosaic appetites. These are perhaps symbolized by its greatest writer, François Rabelais, who was born near the old town of Chinon, where his father was a lawyer. Although the adjective Rabelaisian has overtones of coarseness, the pleasure to be gained from simply eating and drinking in this part of France is enormous. Its wines are wonderful and the food can be magnificent.

The wines of the Loire valley are often thought to be mainly dry whites. The best known of these is Muscadet, which goes so well with fish, but other favourites are Pouilly-Fumé,

Savennières, the flowery Sancerre and the sparkling whites of Vouvray. Many other varieties are equally worth drinking, such as the excellent Sauvignon de Touraine. Less well known, and a lovely surprise, are the red wines of the region. Saumur Champigny never lets you down, while experts speak highly of the refreshing Chinon, Bourgueil and St Nicholas de Bourgueil. One of the great liqueurs, Cointreau, comes from Angers.

Local specialities include the soft goats' milk cheese from Sainte-Maure. The classic creamy sauce known as *beurre blanc*, made from butter warmed and flavoured with wine, vinegar and shallots, was created on the Loire and makes a perfect accompaniment to the local fish, including pike (*brochet au beurre blanc*). The Loire is a salmon river and there is little to touch the taste of fresh salmon, especially *saumon en papillotte*, in which the fish is cooked in buttered paper so that it remains delightfully moist. Trout in white wine and *quenelles* of conger eel are other delicacies. Chicken is cooked in many delectable ways, including *coq au vin* using the red wine of Chinon.

It is difficult to avoid mushrooms in one form or another, perhaps stuffed or served in a cream sauce, since growers in Saumur produce three-quarters of the national crop. The delicious fungi are nurtured in extensive underground galleries that are old quarry workings. The caves were also used by wine growers, with the grapes being tipped down holes in the rock to the wine-presses beneath.

Sea breezes, blowing in from the Atlantic, bring a breath of fresh air to the often sticky climate and turn the sails of a fleet of windmills. The summers can be very hot, particularly in July and August; May and June and possibly September are the best months to visit if you plan to do any strenuous cycling. The height of the summer, too, brings crowds of tourists, although these can be avoided by keeping away from the well-trodden routes.

Away from the tourist centres the locals are friendly and helpful. One pair of cyclists who paused at a crossroads to try to work out the best route to their hotel were surprised when a lorry drew up on the other side of the road. The driver got out and came over. 'You want to know the best way?' he said, 'I will show you the easiest way.' Then he loaded their bikes on to the back of his lorry and gave them a lift into town! Another couple who stopped for a rest at Fosse-Bellay south of Saumur began to talk to a farmer and his wife and in no time found themselves being shown the vineyard and vegetable garden, introduced to the seven grandchildren and invited to drink a bottle of wine.

The Loire is a gently-flowing river that idles its way through fertile, glorious country. On its banks the châteaux mirror the history of the land, from the grim fortresses of the Middle Ages to the magical palaces of the 17th and 18th centuries. There are so many of them that it can be difficult deciding which to visit and which to leave for another time. Often, though, they are best seen from the outside, mirrored in the waters of the river or set amid woods and green fields. Inside, many can be disappointing, with furniture that suggests a shabby present rather than their magnificent past.

Everywhere the past is all around you, one that is inextricably interwoven with the heritage of Britain, for the Loire was more familiar to the fierce and restless Angevin kings of England— Henry II (1133–89), Richard I (1157–99) and John (1167–1216)—than the Thames. Henry, born at le Mans, was not only king of England; he was also Count of Anjou-Maine (roughly equivalent to the department of Maine et Loire) and Duke of Normandy and Aquitaine. His wife, the remarkable Eleanor, Duchess of Aquitaine (1122–1204), married him two months after she was divorced by Louis VII of France. She probably regretted it, for she later led a rebellion against him and, as a result, was kept under house-arrest for 16 years. The marriage gave Henry possession of virtually all western France, a larger territory than the French king. Five generations later this union was to usher in the Hundred Years War (1337–1453) through the actions of their great-great-great-grandson Edward III.

Henry's mother was Matilda, granddaughter of William the Conqueror and a widowed empress when she married the 15-year-old Geoffroy, Count of Anjou (1113–50). This boy was the first of the English Plantagenet kings, so-called because of his habit of wearing a branch of broom (*planta genista* in Latin, *genet* in French) on his helmet, a shrub which grows wild in Anjou.

Henry was to prove one of the greatest of English kings, but although he took possession of his French territories when his father died, he had to wait a while before succeeding to the English throne. His court would move from one great city of the Loire to another, settling for instance at le Mans, Nantes, Chinon, Caen and Saumur. Angers was as much the centre of Plantagenet power as was London, and Henry built many of the city's most splendid buildings, including the Hospital Saint-Jean, with its high arches, the cathedral of Saint-Maurice, and the churches of Saint-Serge, the Trinity and Saint-Martin. The hallmark of this Angevin architecture is its splendid vaulting.

Not far from Angers, at Montmirail, he and the intransigent and violent Archbishop Thomas Becket met in a bungled attempt to reconcile their differences. As part of his public repentance following the murder of Becket at Canterbury Cathedral, Henry founded the Carthusian monastery at le Liget and the priory of Pommiers-Aigres at Saint-Benoît-la-Forêt. Many of the châteaux in the area had fallen to him in his days of glory. But he died at Chinon, a bitter and defeated man, destroyed in a rebellion led by his favourite son John. Later, the body of another son, Richard (Richard the Lionheart), more warrior than king, was also brought to Chinon.

John, a cunning and treacherous man, had attempted to usurp Richard's throne before succeeding him after his brother was killed near Limoges, shot by a stray bolt from a crossbow. In the endless dynastic struggles of the time John had lost his lands in the Loire by alienating most of his supporters, not least through brutally murdering his nephew Arthur (whom Richard had once wanted to succeed him as king of England).

The tombs of these passionate monarchs are at the massive Abbey of Fontevraud, west of Chinon, the site of five separate monasteries. You can see the effigies of Henry II and his queen, Eleanor of Aquitaine, carved from stone, and their son Richard lies close by. Here too is the lovely wooden tomb of Isabelle of Angoulême, praised for her beauty. At about the age of 12, she was abducted by Richard's brother John, who married her and made her queen of England. On his death, however, she returned to France, married the man to whom she had been betrothed as a young girl and meddled so unsuccessfully in the politics of the time that she was forced to flee to live with the nuns at Fontevraud, where she died. Her son Henry III, visiting her grave from England, had her body removed from the cemetery into the church and ordered that a tomb was built over it. His heart and

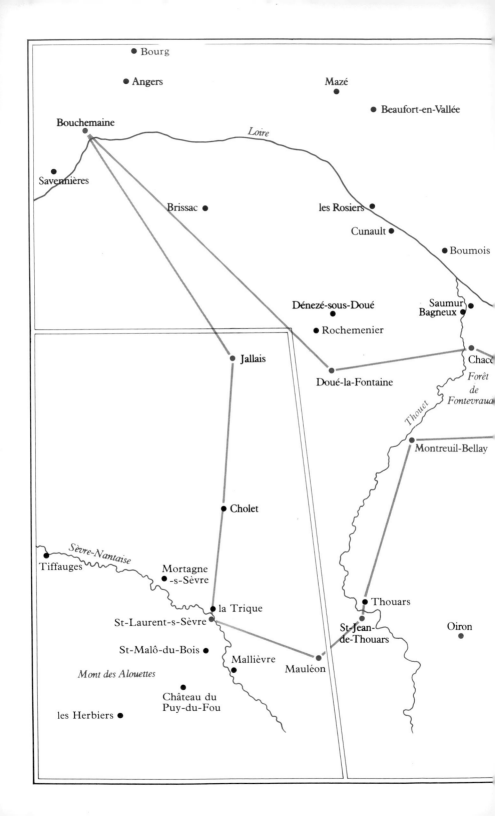

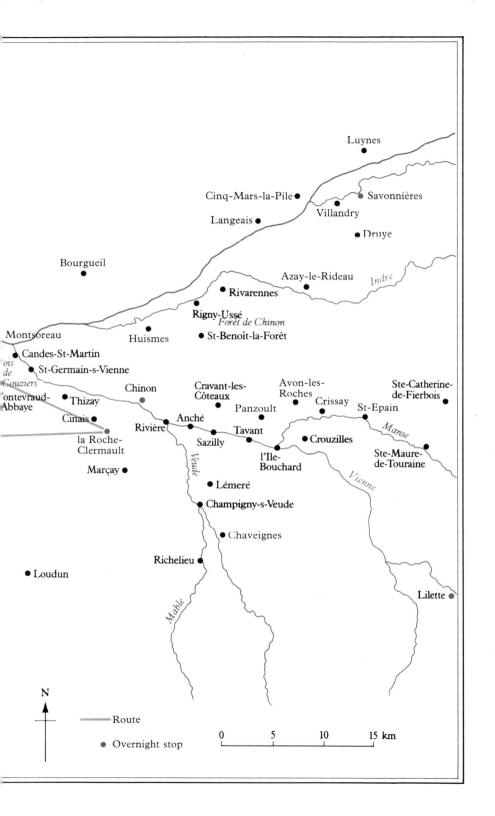

that of John were buried in the abbey's crypt.

Fontevraud should not be missed by anyone with an interest in English history—or, possibly, in French literature, for in modern times it became the prison where Jean Genet, playwright and novelist, was incarcerated. It is only in the last 25 years that it has begun to be restored. Its future remains a matter of controversy now that it is owned by a commercial organization who, some fear, may try to turn it into a sort of Gallic Disneyland.

There are two approaches to touring the region. One is to stay in a central town and make trips out each day to the surrounding countryside. The other is to move on from place to place. Both have their attractions, depending on how far you wish to cycle in a day.

My tours of the region start from Montreuil-Bellay, a small, quiet town dating from the Middle Ages which lies 15 km south of Saumur on the river Thouet. Its château, which has an interior as exciting as its exterior, was partly demolished on the orders of Henry II's father, Geoffroy Plantagenet, after its owner had defied him. The massive fortifications and high-ceilinged rooms of the present building date from the 15th century and are well worth a visit, although the château is closed every Tuesday, the town's market day. Montreuil-Bellay also still has three of its medieval fortified gateways.

The Splendid Hôtel in the rue du Docteur Gaudrez is an excellent centre for a cycling holiday. Its owners, M. and Mme Berville, are tremendous hosts and enormous fun. A fortnight's gentle cycling from here through little-visited areas could take in overnight stops at Thouars, Mauléon, Saint-Laurent, Jallais, Bouchemaine, Doué, Chacé and la Roche-Clermault.

Thouars is 20 km to the south straight down the D938, but it is much more pleasurable to take a longer route through the country on either side. A stronghold in the Middle Ages, some of Thouars' fortifications still remain. The château is now a boys' school. James I of Scotland's daughter Margaret (1424–44), a poet and the unhappy wife of Louis XI, whom she married at Tours, is buried in Saint-Laon, a former abbey church which she had built. Louis XI stayed in the Hôtel des Trois Rois, one of the oldest houses in the town. At the Tour de Prince de Galles, which dates back to the 12th century, you can see the wooden cages, built in the 1600s, where criminals were kept.

We stay just outside the town, at Saint-Jean-de-Thouars. The Hôtel du Château here is run by the exuberant M. Ramard, who has an inexhaustible fund of knowledge and advice about the local wines.

A gentle outing from here would be to cycle 13 km to Oiron (pronounced 'Waaron')—take the D759 towards Loudun and then turn right on to the D162. Oiron is the site of one of the great renaissance châteaux of France, built by the Comte de Caravas who served as a model for the Comte de Carabas in *Puss in Boots*. Louis XIV's mistress Madame de Montespan lived there after she was replaced in the royal affections. In the main square is the Relais du Château, a tiny *auberge* serving delicious meals. Some 9 km to the south, along the D64, is the highly decorated church of Saint-Jouin-de-Marnes, where there is also a lake in which you can swim.

From Thouars, take the D759 westward to cycle the 45 km to Mauléon, a small country town. The Hôtel de l'Europe, run by M. Michel Lemercier, is a typical rural establishment with an excellent restaurant. The town, which has a market day on Friday, has an interesting church and abbey.

West of Mauléon, 13 km along the N149, is Saint-Laurent-sur Sèvre, a charming small town on the river Sèvre-Nantaise. If you are thinking of having a picnic, seek out the delicacies in the *charcuterie* here. You could go straight on to Cholet, 11 km north on the D752, and then another 17 km to Jallais, taking the D752

north of Cholet and turning right on to the D15, but it is worth
lingering to enjoy the tranquillity of the countryside.
L'Hermitage Hôtel in Saint-Laurent can be recommended.

A *son-et-lumière* staged near Saint-Laurent uses actors from
the local communities. It takes place at a ruined château at Puy-
du-Fou during June and July, and from mid August to the end of
the month. You can travel by steam train from Mortagne-sur-
Sèvre (5 km away on the N149) on the line south to les Herbiers
to see the show.

You can also take a delightful ride west along the river valley
to Tiffauges 20 km away, where there are the ruins of the château
that was the home of Gilles de Rais (1404–40), better known as
the appallingly sadistic Bluebeard. He fought at the side of Joan
of Arc and was a marshal of France before his notorious
retirement to the château to indulge in the vile orgies that
climaxed in the murder of maybe as many as 200 young boys.
Tried for his crimes at Nantes, he was hanged and burned there.

One of the highest spots in the area is the Mont des Alouettes,
15 km to the south-west of Saint-Laurent along winding lanes,
or 20 km if you turn left at Mortagne-sur-Sèvre and travel down
the main N160. The windmills here were used to send signals
across the countryside during the local wars of the 1790s that
followed the French Revolution.

Les Bois de la Boulaye, the château at Mallièvre, was the
headquarters of one of the armies involved. Unfortunately, it is
not open to visitors, but Mallièvre itself is worth exploring.
Buried in the countryside, old houses lean over ancient streets
and a gently crumbling watermill stands by a small stream. It is
8 km from Saint-Laurent—travel south along the D752 to Saint-
Malô-du-Bois and then turn left on to the D72. If gastronomy is
of greater interest than history, then make a detour to la Trique,
2 km to the north of Saint-Laurent along the D752, where the
Restaurant la Chaumière is well worth a visit.

Cholet to the north is probably best avoided on a Saturday, when there is a huge cattle market, but it has two interesting museums. The Musée des Guerres de Vendée commemorates the destruction of the town during the revolutionary period of the 1790s. The Musée des Beaux-Arts, housed in an 18th-century building, has work by many French artists, including Toulouse-Lautrec and Matisse.

At Jallais, the Hôtel la Croix Verte in the centre of the town has an excellent restaurant and is a good place to stay. Market day there is on a Friday. Then go on to Bouchemaine, 40 km north-east by the D15, D762 and D111. This is a tiny village just outside Angers with an especially good restaurant at the Hôtel l'Ancre de Marine, where M. Bernhard Proust can advise on what is best to eat that day, and where overnighters are made very welcome.

Angers, the centre of Plantagenet power in the 12th century, is then only 7 km away. Traces of its former importance can still be seen in this bustling town, which today is perhaps better known as the place where the liqueur Cointreau is made. It is a city full of flowers, its streets lined by camellias and magnolia trees. The cathedral of Saint-Maurice is a masterpiece of vaulted Angevin architecture. The château dates from the mid 1200s, after the French had regained possession of the town from John, and is a magnificent fortress with 17 towers. It houses a collection of many of the world's finest tapestries, including the oldest surviving medieval example, the Apocalypse tapestry, woven in the 1370s and depicting the revelation of St John the Divine.

More recent but none the less beautiful tapestry-work is to be found in the ancient Hospital of Saint-Jean, which dates back to the time of Henry II and is another example of splendid Angevin vaulting. It contains the huge series of tapestries known as *The Song of the World* created by Jean Lurçat (1892–1966), who was responsible for reviving this ancient art.

Savennières, a small town with a charming church 6 km to the south-west of Bouchemaine, reached along a road that runs beside the Loire, has the best vineyards in Anjou. So do sample the local wine if you get a chance.

Fine châteaux in the area include the château of Plessis-Bourré (see p.25), 22 km north of Angers. Take the D107 to Bourg, turn right on to the D108 and left on to the D508. From Plessis-Bourré there is an enjoyable cross-country ride to the château of Plessis-Macé, 13 km north-west of Angers. Louis XI sometimes stayed in this moated manor house.

Another fine moated building is the Château de Serrant, 16 km south-west of Angers, which stands in a magical setting, with its wide moat and lake reflecting the renaissance building. There is some excellent furniture inside, but the greatest pleasure of visiting this enchanting spot is to sit by the lakeside, sipping the local white wine, probably the best of its kind in Anjou. The château was once owned by an Irishman, Anthony Walsh, who was a supporter of Bonnie Prince Charlie. Portraits of both can be seen in the library.

From Bouchemaine, cycle south-east for 40 km on the D748 and D83 to Doué-la-Fontaine. This route takes you past the towering seven storeys of the château at Brissac after 15 km. Its two ivy-covered towers date back to the 15th century, but the main building between them was built in the 17th century. Although it has 150 rooms, it was never finished. The same family has occupied it for more than 500 years and have kept it much as it was. It is still magnificent, with Flanders, Brussels and Gobelin tapestries on the walls, and gilded ceilings.

The old town of Doué is a rose-grower's paradise, set in fascinating limestone country where houses have been carved out of the stone and some of the many quarries transformed to other uses. The Zoo des Minières on the D960 towards Cholet has used quarries to house its inhabitants—one contains emus, another forms a large aviary full of birds of prey. Monkeys and birds wander freely around the place. In the town itself, seats were carved from the stone in another quarry 500 years ago to create an arena which is used as an open-air theatre and concert hall.

More extraordinary are the region's troglodyte homes. Some were formed in caves in the cliffs but others were dug underground, set around a sunken courtyard. The troglodytes, or cave-dwellers, only gave up such homes in the last 50 years. About 6 km north of Doué-la-Fontaine is the troglodyte village of Rochemenier, which once had a large concentration of such dwellings. The underground village was bigger than the one now visible on the surface. Two underground farms and store-rooms, as well as a subterranean chapel, are open to visitors.

Another sight of the region is the cave at Dénezé-sous-Doué, just to the north of Rochemenier along the D69, where the walls are covered with fantastic carvings of people, thought to have been made in the 1500s.

The Hôtel de France in the centre of Doué, by the large square that houses the Monday market, can be recommended. The town is surrounded by vineyards and the local wine, a pleasant accompaniment to a picnic, can be bought very cheaply straight from the farms.

South of Doué the church of le-Puy-Notre-Dame, 9 km away down the D87, houses a relic of the Virgin's belt, said to have been brought there from Jerusalem 800 years ago. The church itself is a fine example of Angevin architecture. From here you could go north to the Abbaye d'Asnière, 8 km to the east of Doué, a ruined 12th-century monastery set in forested country.

From Doué, take the D960 towards Saumur for 15 km, turn right on the D160 for 4 km following the river Thouet, and then left over the river, and you arrive at Chacé. This small village is only 5 km from Saumur, away from the noise and bustle of the larger town but near enough to make it easy to visit it and its many attractions. The Auberge de Thouet can be recommended.

Saumur was once a bigger and more prosperous town than it is today, though it is vigorous enough. A centre of the Protestant faith, many of its inhabitants left after they lost their rights in the 1680s with the Revocation of the Edict of Nantes. The Loire is divided by an island here and seems to be two separate rivers. The town itself is mostly built on a long finger of land between the Loire and its tributary the Thouet. The great château of Saumur rises menacingly from a hilltop above the town, its crenellations, pepper-pot towers and massive walls recalling an illustration in a medieval manuscript. Built at the end of the 14th century, on the site of an earlier castle, it became a prison in the last century, but more recently has been restored to some of its former glory.

It houses two museums, the Musée des Arts Decoratifs, which contains furniture and tapestries, and the Musée du Cheval, which is devoted to horses, commemorating the town's famous cavalry school. Although the cavalry has been replaced by armoured cars, the Cadre Noir team of the National Riding School still give displays of their horsemanship on the first Friday of each month. The Riding School has its own cavalry museum and there is also a tank museum that contains clanking machines from several countries involved in the Second World War.

Saumur produces masses of mushrooms and a dry, white, sparkling wine, named after the town, which Henry II brought over to England. Other local wines are the rosé Cabernet de Saumur and the red Saumur Champigny. Return to Chacé from Saumur by the N147 and D160, a route which takes you through Bagneux to the south. The astounding megalithic way here is a 20 metre tunnel formed from massive stones.

On the northern bank of the Loire, 20 km east of Saumur, Bourgueil produces a very drinkable wine, mentioned by Rabelais and known locally as Breton, though it has no connection with Brittany. You can sample it at the Cave de la Dive Bouteille, a wine museum just north of the town. Bourgueil also has an imposing arcaded market-place and a fortified Benedictine abbey.

Some 30 km north-west of Saumur, off the N147 at Mazé and along the D74, is the remarkable Château de Montgeoffroy, which has stood virtually unchanged since it was built and furnished in 1772. Thanks to the fact that it has remained in the possession of the family that built it, the rooms still contain the original furniture that was designed for them, as well as paintings by some of the leading artists of the day. The restrained classical building with a white façade, slate roof and pink brick chimneys is framed by two towers remaining from an earlier château. Montgeoffroy is open from March until October. Some 8 km before you reach it, Beaufort-en-Vallée is a small, ancient town with a ruined castle from which there are splendid views across the rich countryside.

From Saumur take the D751 for a lovely ride downstream along the bank of the Loire for 15 km to Cunault. The remarkable church here was built over a couple of centuries from the 1000s. It is on a massive scale and was once the centre of a thriving Benedictine monastery. Go on downstream to Gennes, cross the river to les Rosiers and come back along the opposite bank to Boumois, where a small château stands by the Loire. Built in the 1590s and early 1600s, it shows the transition from gothic to early renaissance styles. The scenic D229 leads back to Saumur.

East from Saumur there are enchanting back roads through the Forêt de Fontevraud and the Bois de Couziers to the last stop on the tour, la Roche-Clermault, a small village close to Chinon. If you don't mind cycling uphill, the Auberge du Haut Clos,

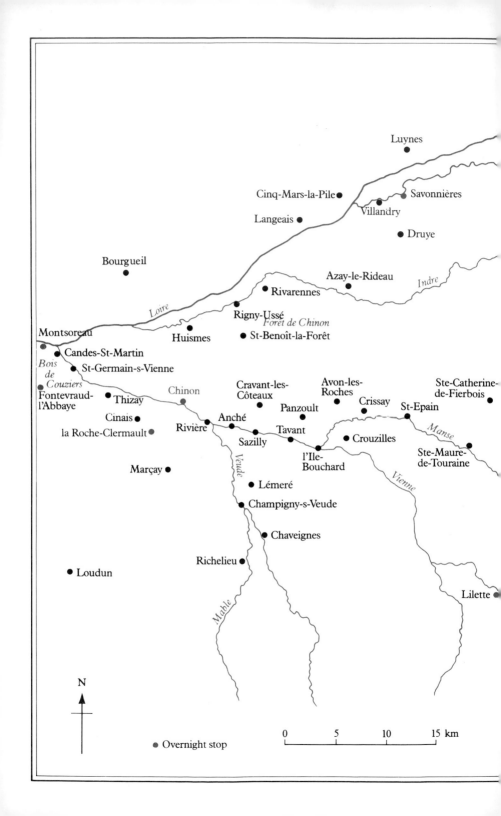

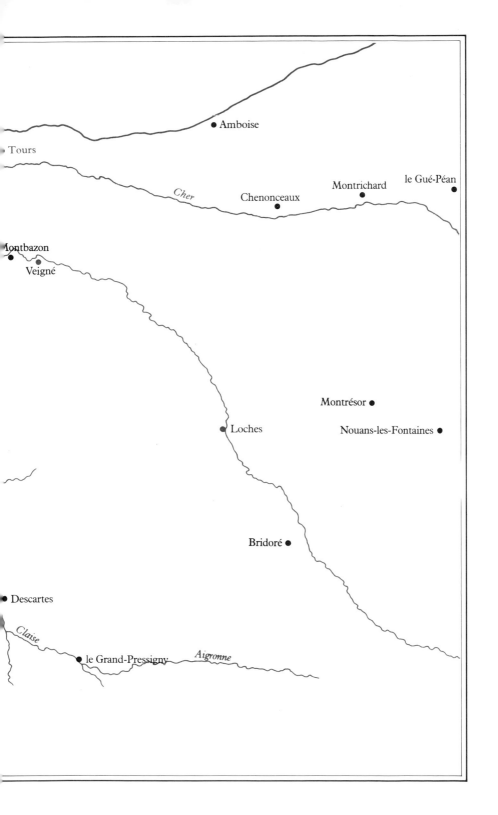

reached by a steep, windy road off the D759 south of Chinon, is recommended. The views from here are superb, and you could use it as a base from which to explore the châteaux of Ussé and Villandry on the Loire to the north (see pp.64 and 73), as well as Fontevraud to the west (see p.49).

If you prefer to set out each day from the same place, two cities provide particularly good centres for touring in the Loire: Tours and Chinon (which is twinned with the Devon town of Tiverton). From Tours, you can explore not only the Loire itself, since the town stands on the river, but the valleys of two of its tributaries, the Cher and the Indre. Chinon is built on another tributary, the Vienne, but is also close to the Thouet, which joins the Loire just downstream. Both tributaries provide rides through glorious countryside to fascinating towns and châteaux.

These days Tours is a busy industrial city, though it manages to conceal the fact well enough. It still retains some splendid old houses and medieval alleys. It was once famous for its silk and the local weavers' work can still be seen in the city's silk museum. The centre of the old city was built around the tomb of St Martin, bishop of Tours in the late 300s, which was associated with miraculous happenings and became a place of pilgrimage. The basilica of Saint-Martin, built in the last century, now covers the site of his tomb, which was lost after the original building was damaged during the Revolution and then destroyed.

Also gone is the castle Henry II built, where Joan of Arc came after her victory at Orléans to be received by Charles VII. The cathedral of Saint-Gatien, begun in the 1100s and not finished for 400 years, contains the tombs of the children of Charles VIII and Anne of Brittany. Balzac set his novel *The Curé of Tours* in the cathedral close. The magnificent Archbishop's Palace is now an art museum that contains two of the finest paintings by the precocious Italian Andrea Mantegna. In its courtyard is a cedar of Lebanon planted in 1808.

Tours is also associated with Pierre de Ronsard (1524–85). The greatest French poet of his time, he turned to literature when deafness ended his chance of a career as a soldier and diplomat. This remarkable man is buried where he died in arthritic agony, at the city's priory of Saint-Cosme, one of the abbeys granted him by his king. The wines of Touraine are celebrated in a museum housed in the cellar of the ruined abbey of Saint-Julien.

There is a good choice of hotels in Tours itself, but there are also pleasant places to stay just outside for those who prefer to be away from the noise and bustle of the city. At Veigné, 9 km south of Tours on the D50, Le Moulin Fleuri is an old mill transformed into an excellent small hotel, with a patio that looks over the Indre. Near Savonnières, 12 km west of Tours on the D7, the Ferme la Martinière is a simple *chambres d'hôte*, where the farm buildings have been converted into comfortable bedrooms. The road between Savonnières and la Martinière is very steep, so it is best approached from the village of Druye.

It would take a real cycling enthusiast to see all the châteaux in Touraine (at the last count there were 26 that you could view), but the finest are within riding distance of Tours. Most of the châteaux open to the public lie to the west or east of the town. Many are within 20 km or so. If you are energetic, two round trips of some 50 km would enable you to visit the most splendid examples. Go west on the north bank of the Loire for 23 km from Tours along the N152, which will take you through Luynes, Cinq-Mars-la-Pile and Langeais. Luynes, a small village clinging to the side of a hill just off the main road, has a medieval castle. Cinq-Mars-la-Pile is another ancient village, with a curious Gallo-Roman tower 30 metres high of unknown purpose. The ruins of its château date from the 1200s and it is well worth climbing the remaining towers to get a spectacular view across the valley.

The Château de Langeais, in the centre of the town, was built in the 15th century and has been hardly altered since. Its *donjon*, or keep, was virtually impregnable and was cut off from the rest of the building, although there is now a passageway to it. This forbidding fortress has a covered runway at rooftop level from which the defendants, safe from harm, could drop anything from stones to boiling oil on their attackers. Here Charles VIII, known as 'the affable', was married to Anne of Brittany in 1491. The interior is full of furniture and decoration of the period.

At Langeais, you cross the bridge to the south bank of the Loire. At this point there are alternative routes back to Tours. The first takes you along the D7, which runs near the river.

The attraction to the east is the Château de Villandry. Built in the mid 1500s, it is the last of the great renaissance châteaux of the Loire valley. It includes a keep of an earlier period, which gives it a slightly incongruous appearance. But the glory of Villandry is its gardens, restored to their original 16th-century state earlier this century. They are on three levels. On the first the waters of the Cher are tamed into lakes and fountains. Then comes an ornamental garden divided into flower-filled geometric shapes by low hedges and gravel walks. Finally, there is an elaborate vegetable garden. The château, which has an 18th-century interior, is open from mid March to early November, but the gardens remain open all year.

Cycling on towards Tours along the D7 for another 3 km brings you to the Caves-Gouttières of Savonnières, with grottoes full of stalactites and stalagmites. Then, on the outskirts of the city, is the Château de Plessis-les-Tours, where Louis XI spent his happiest days.

After crossing the bridge at Langeais, you could also continue along the D57 to Azay-le-Rideau in the valley of the Indre, where there is a spectacular château. In its present form it dates from the early 1500s and was built for effect rather than defence. Very effective it looks, too—an imposing building in a beautiful setting with its gothic pinnacles and windows mirrored in the lake. The interior is set out as a museum of the renaissance. During the summer there is *son-et-lumière* every evening. The far more modest Château Saché, 6 km east along the D17 on the opposite bank of the river, was often visited by Balzac, who wrote *Le Père Goriot* and *Le Lys dans la Vallée* there in the mid 1830s. His study is exactly as it was then and the house is full of mementoes of his life.

Continue along the D17 for another 15 km, with the road winding beside the Indre, and you come to Montbazon, with its ruined castle built in the 1000s. From there it is a quick 9 km ride back to Tours, while Veigné is only five minutes away.

Three of the finest châteaux are all to be found to the east of Tours—Amboise (25 km), Chenonceaux (30 km) and Chambord (70 km). Louis XI and Charles VIII lavished much care in building the Château d'Amboise beside the Loire, although perhaps not as much as they should, since Charles died after cracking his head against the low lintel of one of the castle's doorways. François I, who lived there during the first years of his reign in the early 1500s, invited Leonardo da Vinci to Amboise and gave him the nearby manor of Clos-Lucé to live in (now 600 metres from the city centre). Da Vinci died there and was buried in the collegiate church that was destroyed during the Revolution. Last century his remains were reburied in the gothic chapel dedicated to St Hubert, added to the château by Charles VIII in the 1490s. The red-brick manor house where Leonardo lived is now a museum containing models of his many amazing inventions.

Amboise itself continues to have royalist connections. The Comte de Paris, pretender to the French throne, installed his grandson, Prince Jean d'Orléans, as the Dauphin in a ceremony at the château in 1987. This culminated in a sumptuous dinner featuring salmon from the Loire, accompanied by the red and rosé wines of Amboise.

For the really energetic and culture enthusiasts the largest renaissance château in France is 40 km north-east of Amboise: the massive white-stone Château de Chambord, built at great expense by François I and Henri II in the mid 1500s. Now surrounded by a 14,000-acre walled wildlife reserve, it has 440 rooms, 365 chimneys and 74 staircases. It was later a favourite haunt of Louis XIV. During his reign what is now called a guardroom, and was earlier a billiard room, was used as a theatre. It was the scene of the first performance of Molière's comedies *Monsieur de Pourceaugnac* and *Le Bourgeois Gentilhomme*, neither of which seemed to have much amused the king when he saw them.

Cycle south across country from Amboise on the D81 to one of the most beautiful of castles, the Château de Chenonceaux. This was built in the early 1500s over the river Cher, replacing a mill that once stood on the site. The château was actually constructed across the river itself, standing on six graceful arches. It, too, has many royal associations. Henri II of France installed his mistress Diane de Poitiers there, until his widow Catherine de' Medici claimed it for herself and forced Diane to give it up. The ornamental gardens date from Catherine's time. After Henri III's assassination in 1589, his sorrowing widow Louise de Lorraine lived in the château. In the 18th century Jean-Jacques Rousseau was a tutor there to the son of M. Dupin and the *salon* established by Mme Dupin attracted many of the leading wits and intellectuals of the day. From June to September there is a nightly *son-et-lumière* presenting its history.

Go on another 21 km east through Montrichard and left on to the D21 to the Château du Gué-Péan, open all the year round. The entrance looks forbidding, but inside it is more like a country house, built around a central courtyard with an ornamental pond in the middle. The château contains Louis XV and Louis XVI furniture, some fine tapestries and paintings. You can picnic in the grounds. Montrichard itself has a ruined castle dating from the 1100s that now houses a folk museum.

North of Tours, 7 km along the N10, is the huge Grange de Meslay, a fortified farm dating from the 1200s. A longer but more pleasant route to it is by the D77.

There are also places worth visiting to the south on the N10. A 23 km ride from Veigné will bring you to the hamlet of Sainte-Catherine-de-Fierbois, which has associations with Joan of Arc. A few kilometres further on Sainte-Maure-de-Touraine is a small town that dates from Roman times, although there are also prehistoric remains in the area. It has an attractive covered market, built in the 1670s, which is entered by two huge doors that were defaced at the time of the Revolution. Part of the market now forms the town hall, which was built in the 1600s; the remainder is still used as a market on Fridays. The church, much altered over the years, was first built in the 1060s.

Directly east along the D760 is the ancient town of Loches, also connected with Joan of Arc. Henry II and his son Richard the Lionheart both lived at its château, creating an almost impregnable fortress. Richard loved it so much that his first action after being released from an Austrian prison was to take it away from the French who had recaptured it. It was built and rebuilt many times. Loches became infamous as the site of a grim royal prison, from which few ever emerged. In its Round Tower was a torture chamber where prisoners were hung in wooden cages.

Joan of Arc came to the château in 1429 to persuade the Dauphin, later Charles VII, to be crowned at Reims. When king, Charles subsequently installed his beautiful mistress Agnès Sorel here. You can see her alabaster effigy, guarded by two angels, in the monastery church. For those who feel they have been far enough for one day, the medieval city contains a delightful old hotel, the Hôtel George Sand, full of mellow stone inside and out and overlooking the river Indre. Perhaps George Sand once stayed here on her way to her house at Nohant-Vic to the south. Otherwise Tours is 35 km away along the N143.

If you do stay in Loches, there are a number of places worth exploring from here. Bridoré, 18 km to the south just off the D41, is notable for its 15th-century fortress fringed on three sides by a deep moat that no longer contains water. It is not open to the public, but is very scenic.

East of Loches, 20 km along the D760, is the château of Montrésor. The walls belong to a fortress built in the eleventh century, but they enclose a manor house dating from the early 1500s. The furnishings reflect the taste of a Polish aristocrat who restored it in the 1850s. A further 9 km on the same road the old church in the small village of Nouans-les-Fontaines contains a masterpiece from the late 1400s—a large painting on wood depicting Christ being taken down from the cross. The artist was Jean Fouquet, the greatest French painter of the Renaissance, who was born at Tours. North-east of Loches, 20 km along the D764, the massive towers of the Château de Montpoupon date from the 13th century, although the remainder of the building is 15th century.

Chinon is a quieter city than Tours and there are several good hotels. The Hôtel Diderot, set back from the Quai Jeanne d'Arc, is a stylish building grouped around a courtyard, where the stables have been turned into bedrooms. It has no restaurant, but there is a lovely breakfast room. Nearby is the Grand Hôtel de la Boule d'Or.

With its three ruined châteaux, Chinon itself is one of the most fascinating of places. This was the town that saw the end to English claims to France, for it was here that Joan of Arc first met the Dauphin, picking him out from his courtiers in 1429 at the Château de Milieu. Nearby is the second château, the moated Château du Coudray, now approached over a stone bridge, where she stayed. And at the third, the Fort Saint-George, Henry II died in bitterness, comforted only by his natural son Geoffrey as his heirs rebelled against him.

It is possible that another English king, Richard the Lionheart, died in one of the medieval houses in the Grand Carroi that still stand today. Certainly he was brought to the town after being shot during a siege at Chalus, where he had gone in search of a fabulous treasure of twelve gold knights sitting at a round table.

As a young man, Rabelais lived in the old part of the town. He was born some 7 km away, at the manor house of la Devinière (reached by the scenic D117), where you can still see his room and a museum devoted to his life and books. The house is small, overlooking a courtyard with a well. The staircase to the first floor is outside the house, shielded by an overhanging porch. It leads to the great writer's parents' room, with its 400-year-old four-poster bed, and to the room where Rabelais slept. Here the date April 8, 1509 on the wall by the window might have been scratched by him when he was 15 years old.

The local red wine is worth sampling and Chinon has an abundance of good restaurants and tea-shops, including the Bonbonnière on the banks of the Vienne. Eleven km to the north-west of the town is a more modern monument: the Avoine-Chinon Centrale Nucleaire, France's first nuclear-powered electricity generating station.

From Chinon, ride due west along the banks of the Vienne towards the small fishing village of Candes-Saint-Martin, a distance of 14 km. Along the way you will pass Cinais. There is a so-called Roman camp here but it is actually the remains of a Gallic settlement. Thizay a few kilometres further on has prehistoric remains. If you are interested in churches, Saint-Germain-sur-Vienne, just outside Candes, has an interesting romanesque example, with beautiful arched vaults.

Candes stands at the meeting-point of the Loire and Vienne

and this too is a village with a remarkable church. It is a massive 13th-century fortified building, marking the spot where St Martin, the Roman legionary who became the miraculous Bishop of Tours, died in 397.

About 2 km further to the west along the Loire is the château of Montsoreau. Built in the 1440s, it features in Alexandre Dumas' novel of unhappy love, *La Dame de Montsoreau*. In a little street behind the château is the Hôtel le Bussy, with its restaurant Hostellerie Diane de Meridor at the bottom of the hill (it is closed on Tuesdays during June and September). You can swim in the Loire here. Just outside the town is the Moulin de la Herpinière, a windmill dating from the 1400s and surrounded by underground buildings where the miller once lived and stored his goods. Nobody who stays in Montsoreau should fail to visit Fontevraud, 5 km to the south, with its relics of the Plantagenets (see p.49). So far the town's Hôtel la Croix Blanche seems untouched by the growing commercialism surrounding the abbey. Built around a flower-filled courtyard, it is an oasis of quiet calm.

East of Chinon, 15 km along the D749 and 760, is the tiny village of Tavant. The walls of the church here, including those in the crypt, are covered by fascinating frescoes dating from the 1100s. Although there are no outstanding buildings to be seen, there is also a delightful ride east on the other side of the river to Saint-Epain. The route along the D21 runs past woods and streams and small villages.

On the way you could pause in Cravant, where there is a museum of gem-stones and the church dates back to the 900s. The surrounding area is rich in prehistoric remains.

At Panzoult, you can see a dovecote built in the 1600s, when doves provided a welcome variation on the winter menu. From here there is a choice of routes: straight on to Crissay, which is a tiny village of under 200 inhabitants, dominated by the ruins of a

15th-century fortress and with houses from the same period; or along the D221 to Crouzilles, where the church contains some splendid Angevin vaulting. From Crouzilles a little road runs directly north to join the D21 to Crissay.

Whichever route you take, it is worth making a detour from the D21 along the D138 to Avon-les-Roches, which has a 12th-century church. Follow the road to Crissay from there and then turn left after about 1 km to climb the hill to the ruins of the early 16th-century collegiate church of Roches-Tranchelion. There are good views across the valley from here. Then return to the Crissay road and continue on to Saint-Epain. Go a little past Saint-Epain, following the minor road along the river Manse and then branching left downhill, and you will come to the chapel of Notre-Dame de Lorette, carved from the rock in the 1500s.

A two-day tour from Chinon could take you 45 km south-east (along the D749 and D20) to Lilette, a few kilometres from Descartes on a windy back road. Here the friendly little Auberge de l'Islette is an excellent *pension* for an overnight stop. Nearby, 12 km to the south-east along the D42, le Grand Pressigny is a small village in the exquisite valley where the Aigronne and the Claise meet. It was a favoured spot in the Stone Age, judging by the number of remains found locally. These are now exhibited, together with a great variety of fossils, in the local museum housed in the remains of the hilltop château. Some 7 km west of here is the impregnable and massive Château de la Guerche, built by Charles VII.

For the energetic, there is also a round trip south of Chinon to Richelieu and back by different roads. The quickest route is to travel along the D749 all the way, a journey of 40 km in total. Richelieu is well worth visiting. It is an extraordinary place, a piece of aristocratic town planning built on the bank of the Mable by Cardinal Richelieu in 1631 when he was the virtual ruler of France. In its rectangular, fortified plan, the town echoes the layout of the French *bastide*, those remarkable medieval examples of town planning (see p.113). But the architecture is noble and classical, designed for the court who were expected to flock to Richelieu's great château in its monumental park.

Richelieu's contemporary, the brilliant, if frivolous poet Jean de la Fontaine called it 'the most beautiful village in the universe'. The château that Richelieu built with such pride and jealousy, destroying neighbouring houses that might compete with it, is now itself demolished. Many of its stones were used for building material during the last century and the grounds are now a public park. But the town remains, full of splendid houses, particularly along the main street, the Grand Rue. Between May and September a steam train runs the short distance between Chinon and Richelieu if you prefer to use another mode of transport.

A more scenic route would be to take the D116 to Marçay and then to ride on to Champigny-sur-Veude, where there are 16th-century houses and the ruins of a massive château that was among those destroyed by Richelieu. The Sainte-Chapelle survived, thanks to the influence of the Pope. Its splendid stained-glass windows describing the life of St Louis are regarded as the finest of the French Renaissance.

From Champigny, continue south to Richelieu. On the return journey, take the D757 or the minor road which echoes it to the north, turning left to Chaveignes and Champigny. There, take the D114 to Lémeré and the moated medieval fortress of Rivau, where Joan of Arc went in search of horses and weapons for the siege of Orléans. Its ceilings date back to the 15th century.

You can follow the D749 back to Rivière, where the church has some interesting romanesque frescoes, and then continue on the road back to Chinon. Or turn right at the junction of the D749 and D760 and make the short detour to Anché, to view the Château de Bretignolles.

Yet another route to Richelieu would take you along the

D749 to Rivière, and the D760 to Anché, Sazilly, with its Angevin church dating from the end of the 1100s, Tavant, and l'Ile-Bouchard, an old port that sprawls across both sides of the river, before turning on to the D757 which leads through pleasant countryside to Richelieu.

North of Chinon, you can make a pleasant trip of 7 km along the D16 to Huismes, which has a 12th-century church, and then go on another 4 km to visit the château at Rigny-Ussé on the banks of the Indre. The Château d'Ussé looks as if it has been transplanted from the pages of a book of fairy-tales, which is not surprising since it served as the model for the castle in Charles Perrault's *Sleeping Beauty*. Its fortified walls and towers date from the late 1400s when it was built as a fortress; it still has its covered galleries from which boiling liquid or rocks could be dropped on its attackers. Inside the chapel in the grounds is an Aubusson tapestry illustrating the life of Joan of Arc.

From Rigny-Ussé continue on the D7 for 6 km to Rivarennes, and then turn right along the wooded road through the Forest of Chinon and Saint-Benoît-la-Forêt, which brings you back to Chinon.

The valley of the Loire is rightly known as the garden of France. If you can avoid the well-trodden tourist routes you will discover many hidden delights. Other regions may not have the magnificent architecture of this part of France, but they too can match it in unexpected pleasure.

CHAPTER THREE

LA
VENISE
VERTE

SOUTH OF NANTES and inland from la Rochelle is a tiny region of France which is quite unlike anywhere else in the country. Officially known as the Marais Poitevin, this was an area of salt marsh which was drained by a network of canals built in the 12th century. Known familiarly as La Venise Verte—France's green Venice—it is one of the most peaceful and picturesque places I know: a rich, verdant countryside interlaced with tranquil waterways.

The locals still use these smooth, peaceful canals as the main means of transport, ferrying goods and people in their traditional flat-bottomed boats. I could happily spend hours sitting listening to the gentle lapping of the water, watching the dappled sunlight streaming through the leaves of the trees on the bank and being lulled by the slow rhythm of the boatmen as they pole their craft along. The loudest sound is likely to be the flapping wings of one of the many kinds of waterfowl taking off in a sudden scurry or landing on the water. Here you will see extraordinary sights, such as boats with a cow or goat on board, standing patiently watching the willows and poplars go by while being ferried from one pasture to the next.

As you might expect, this is an important area for dairy farming, producing rich butter, cheese and cream from the lush pastures. The canals themselves are the source of some of the region's gastronomic specialities, such as eels, frogs and fish. Among the pleasures of the table are *matelote d'anguilles*, eels cooked in a wine sauce, *mojettes à la maraichine*, kidney beans grown in the swampy areas, and *torteau fromage*, or cheesecake. The local dry white wines are a very pleasant and inexpensive accompaniment to any meal. If you ask for a local wine you are likely to be offered Fiefs-Vendeens or Haut-Poitou or, possibly, the sweeter Vins du Thouarsais, but you can also easily obtain the wines of the Loire valley, which is very close. Two of my favourites are the red Saumur Champigny and the white and sometimes sparkling Savennières.

Away from the canals, fields of golden sunflowers and sweetcorn stretch to the horizon. Although romanesque churches are as common here as elsewhere in south-west France, they seem to be more modest in scale and pleasantly rounded in shape and decoration, in fact altogether charming. The châteaux, too, have the same kind of feel, often being little more than lightly fortified manor houses.

In general, the climate is pleasant, with more than 2000 hours of sunshine a year. It can be hot and sticky in summer, but there are always trees to provide welcome shade and the canals have a generally cooling effect.

The main town of the region is Niort, an old port on the river Sèvre which lies on the eastern edge of the Venise Verte. It dates back to Roman times, and has had a fairly turbulent history ever since. Of the great château built by the river here by Henry II and Richard the Lionheart, at the time these English kings controlled south-west France (see p.48), only the keep still stands—two square towers built in the 1180s joined by a building added in the 1500s. The rest of the fortress, which covered a large area, has vanished over the centuries. What is left now houses a local museum where exhibits include an interesting reconstruction of a peasant's home. Climb up to the ramparts for a good view of the river and the countryside round about.

Other interesting buildings in Niort include the church of Notre-Dame, with its lofty spire more than 75 metres high and its splendidly carved gothic north doorway. Then there is a fortified house, dating from the 1500s, that was once the town hall but now contains the Musée du Pilori, a collection of objects found in local archaeological excavations. There are similarly heterogeneous exhibits in the Musée des Beaux-Arts, including a portrait of Madame de Maintenon, the godly widow of the poet Paul Scarron who became Louis XIV's second wife. She was born in Niort in 1635 when her ne'er-do-well father was in prison here. There are some pleasant old half-timbered houses near the museum which date from the same period as Madame de Maintenon. More prosaically, Niort has long been known for its production of angelica, which you are likely to find featuring in desserts in local restaurants. This fragrant plant was once highly regarded as proof against poison and pestilence, but it is now more commonly used as a flavouring, or candied to decorate cakes and puddings. It is also the basis of the distinctive liqueur Angelique de Niort.

I prefer to stay not in Niort but in the much smaller Saint-Maixent-l'Ecole 24 km to the east, a market town dating from the Middle Ages that is best known for its military college founded in 1879 and where there are still many 16th- and 17th-century houses. The Auberge du Cheval Blanc here is an old coaching inn that has been modernized and extended to include excellent new facilities. It also has a superb restaurant which provides memorable meals. Niort grew up around the abbey founded in the 5th century, but its fine church was largely destroyed in the Wars of Religion apart from an 11th-century doorway and an ancient crypt. Most of the building now dates from the 1670s, and the interior is a masterpiece of Flamboyant gothic architecture. Another old foundation is the church of Saint-Léger, where the crypt dates from the 600s. You can swim in the local pool and the town also has tennis courts and local stables for horse-riding. Market day is Saturday and festivals are held during the first week of June and on 20 June.

If you stay a couple of days in Saint-Maixent, there are several interesting places within easy reach. Niort is a day trip south-west from here, or you could go north on the D938 to Parthenay. This ancient fortified town was on the route trodden by thousands of pilgrims from all over Europe making their way to the shrine of St James at Compostela in northern Spain. You

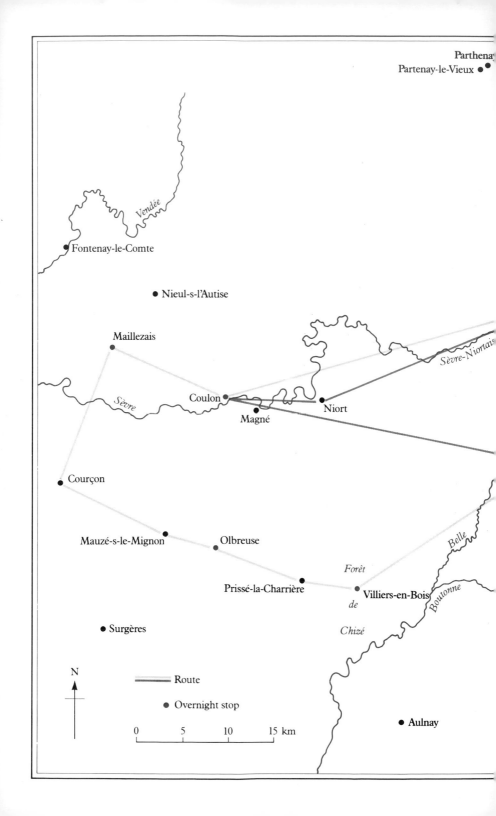

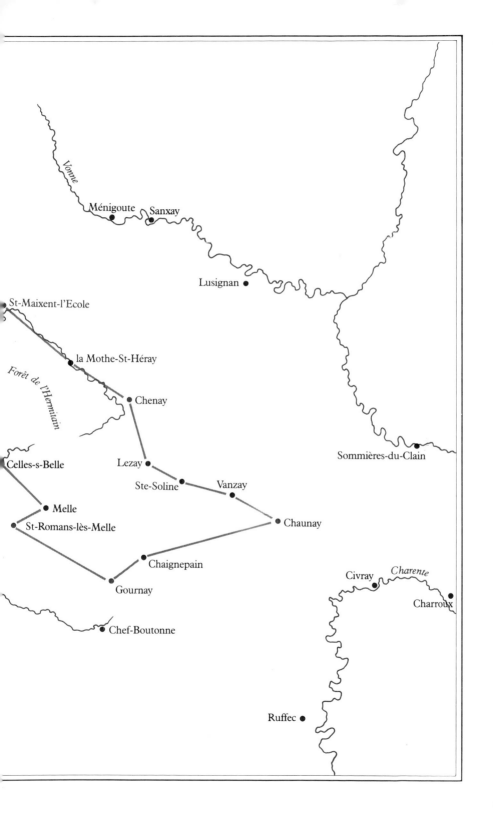

can follow in their footsteps through the Porte-Saint-Jacques, a gateway with two majestic towers standing at one end of an old arched bridge, both dating from the 1100s, and along streets lined with old houses. Just outside the town, at Partenay-le-Vieux on the D743 to Niort, is the 11th-century church of Saint-Pierre, which has a delightful façade and some splendid carvings within.

You could return to Saint-Maixent through Ménigoute down the D21 to the south-east, where there is a charming romanesque chapel. Continuing along the same road for 5 km will bring you to Sanxay, where there are extensive remains of a Roman amphitheatre, baths and a temple. Saint-Maixent is then about 20 km away. This round trip involves a distance of about 70 km and, although it is easy cycling, only the very energetic would want to do it in a day.

With Saint-Maixent as your centre, you could explore the rolling country to the south-east in ten days or a fortnight of easy cycling with overnight stops at Chenay, Chaunay, Gournay, Saint-Romans-lès-Melle and Celles before going west to Coulon. Or you could spend more time in the heart of the Venise Verte, travelling to Coulon, Maillezais, Olbreuse, Villiers and Celles.

Chenay is a small village 20 km south-east of Saint-Maixent. Take the D737 to la Mothe-Saint-Héray, and then the delightful D30 along the beautiful valley of the river Sèvre. Rolling farmland stretches away on either side, and it is possible to cycle for hours and see nobody. The Hôtel les Trois Pigeons at Chenay is one of the most rural places we have found, with bedrooms at the back looking over fields. Le patron cures his own ham and also serves the delicious regional speciality, torteau fromage, which I find irresistible. The hotel's lunch trade is very busy, especially on a Sunday when families sit ten to a table, passing the afternoon eating and drinking.

On the way to Chenay you could pause in la Mothe-Saint-Héray, which has a 15th-century church and the remains of two châteaux, including an orangery. An enchanting ride would be to make your way here along the D10, D103 and D5 from Saint-Maixent, which would take you through the lovely Forêt de l'Hermitain.

North-east of Chenay, 17 km along the D950 an D150, is the old town of Lusignan, built on a hillside overlooking the river Vonne, where you can swim or go boating. Its Promenade de Blossac, laid out in the 1700s, leads to the ruins of the magnificent château which is illustrated in all its glory in *Les Très Riches Heures du duc de Berry*, the famous illuminated manuscript produced in the 14th century. According to legend, the massive walls and high towers of this romantic castle were built in one night by the fairy Mélusine, who became the wife of the local baron. Whether enchanted or not, the barons of Lusignan were very powerful in the Middle Ages, ruling Armenia, Bohemia, Cyprus and Jerusalem. These days the town is dominated by its church of Notre-Dame-et-Saint-Junien, which dates from the 1100s and contains some fascinating carvings of animals.

The next stage of the tour is to Chaunay, 26 km south-east of Chenay. Go south on the D950, and then left along the D45, the D15, D55 and D35 through Lezay (see p.85), Sainte-Soline and Vanzay. The pleasantly old-fashioned Hôtel Central at Chaunay stands in the main street, but thanks to the bypass this is now a back road with only the occasional car. To the south, 20 km along the N10, is the market town of Ruffec, which has several 15th-century houses and a romanesque church. Or cycle south-east to Civray, a charming town on the banks of the Charente with the remarkable church of Saint-Nicolas dating from the 1100s. The figures on its arched façade represent various biblical themes and include nine statues that may be of saints or apostles. Louis XIII and Anne of Austria visited the town just after their marriage in 1615, a union that was to prove profoundly unhappy, and you can still see the house known as the Maison Louis XIII where they stayed.

If you reach Civray, it is worth travelling another 11 km east on the D148 to visit the ruins of the abbey of Saint-Sauveur at Charroux. This great monastery was built in the late 10th century to house a relic of the True Cross, brought back to France by a Crusader, and it became enormously rich and powerful. Although it was almost totally destroyed in the Wars of Religion, its huge octagonal tower still dominates the town. Visit the museum in the chapter-house to see a few of the abbey's former treasures, including some of the statues once on the façade. The village also has a 16th-century market and some medieval houses.

North-east of Chaunay, 16 km along the D25, there is the coldly formal Château de Vareilles at Sommières-du-Clain. Make a detour down the D28 on the way back to see the Château d'Epanvilliers, which can be visited. A fortified manor house built in the 1550s and much altered a hundred years later, it was the home of Madame d'Epanvilliers, who was Louis XV's mistress.

The tour now runs westward again to Gournay, set deep in the countryside, where the elegant Château des Touches is now a hotel run by a former director of the Cordon Bleu School in Paris. It is a ride of 29 km south along the N10 and then west on the D948, turning left at Chaignepain for the final lap.

Six km to the south, the village of Chef-Boutonne marks the source of the river of the same name. Chef-Boutonne is a picturesque place with a 12th-century church and some old houses, known round about for the potted goose produced here. A little to the west of the village is the Château de Javarzay, dating from the 1500s, which has an extraordinary bulbous round tower with a high, pointed roof.

To the north, 13 km along the D105, the market town of Lezay is noted for its goats' milk cheeses and its *torteau fromage*. Herds of brown and white goats are very much a feature of this part of France and you feel transported back in time when you see them grazing by some ancient fortified farmhouse.

From Gournay, the next stop is Saint-Romans-lès-Melle, 13 km north-west on the D301. A tranquil little village with a shop and a church set in the valley of the Béronne, its Chambres d'Hôte is more a guest-house than a hotel where everyone eats *en famille*. It has the bonus of a lovely garden. To find it, take the road to Melle out of the village, turn sharp right and it is on your left.

At Melle itself, 4 km away along the D101, the Romans established silver mines and coins were minted in the town for 300 years from the 7th century. The remains of the mines can be visited in the hills just to the south.

Melle also prospered as a staging-post on the pilgrim route to Compostela and has three churches dating from the 1100s. The most notable is Saint-Hilaire, known particularly for the curious statue above its fine carved north doorway. This shows a man on a horse with an old man seated on the ground in front of him, looking up at the rider. The significance of the group is no longer known. Of the other two 12th-century churches, Saint-Savinien was used as a prison for many years until the 1920s but has now been restored. A music festival is held there during May and June. The church of Saint-Pierre is a plainer, but nicely pro-portioned building.

Melle is on the way to the next stopover, Celles-sur-Belle, which is only 11 km away along the D948. It is another little town which has been saved by its bypass, which means that you can now stand in the square and admire the lovely abbey or the 11th-century church in tranquillity. The Hôtel le National is recommended here.

The final stop is Coulon, which lies 32 km north-west of Celles-sur-Belle. The simplest route is by way of Niort, along the D948 and then along the D9 through Magné. A small village set on the edge of the Venise Verte, Coulon is one of the few places where you can still see a farmer set off in a punt to milk his cows and return some time later with his churn on board. There are two tiny hotels in the village: the Hôtel le Central and the Hôtel au Marais, both of which are recommended. The village church, which dates from the 1000s, is worth a visit and so is the aquarium, where you can see specimens of the fish found in the local rivers and canals. During July, drama and folk groups come to the village for a festival.

Birds, flowers and all kinds of wildlife flourish in this watery countryside. Even the most unfit will be able to cycle along the waterways with ease, but it is also possible to take to the canals in a punt—for an hour or a day. Travelling gently along in these flat-bottomed boats past lush river banks, you can explore backwaters that cannot be reached by road. Or make a day trip to Fontenay-le-Comte, 25 km north-west along the D1 and N148. This small town of old buildings spread along both banks of the river Vendée is known for its many literary associations. In the early 16th century Fontenay was an artistic and intellectual centre of renaissance France, and the satirist François Rabelais became a novice at the monastery here. Some 250 years later the Marquis de Sade wrote his scandalous novel *Justine* in the town and more recently Georges Simenon used it as a setting for his great fictional detective Maigret. Just west of the town, the château of Terre-Neuve is open to the public. From Coulon, Saint-Maixent is a day's journey along the D9 and N11 through Niort.

Alternatively, you could plan a tour even further into the Venise Verte west of Coulon. Cycling first from Saint-Maixent to Coulon, you could then go on to Maillezais, 18 km away along little back roads that follow the canals or wind between them. The whole area is criss-crossed by these waterways, and there are plenty of opportunities to hire punts. The Hostellerie Saint-Nicolas at Maillezais has bedrooms arranged around a little garden at the back of the hotel. It no longer provides dinner but the Restaurant le Collibert opposite can be recommended.

It is difficult to believe that Maillezais was once a place of importance in the world. In the Middle Ages and until the 1600s the dukes of Aquitaine exercised their power from this fortified island, which included a powerful Benedictine abbey as well as a cathedral. After Rabelais was expelled from Fontenay-le-Comte in 1523 for owning subversive books, he fled to the monks there for shelter. Today the 14th-century abbey is only a ruin surrounded by the remains of fortified walls, but you can still see a little cell, known as Rabelais' dungeon, where the monks are said to have confined him when they wearied of his exuberance. They cannot have treated him too harshly, since Rabelais sent the abbey some of the plants and seeds he collected secretly from the pope's garden when he was later in Rome. As a result, the monks are credited with introducing the tomato, the melon and the artichoke into France. They were also responsible for draining the marshes around the island by digging a series of canals, and so formed the delightful area we know today. The 11th-century cathedral is also in ruins but the 12th-century church of Saint-Nicolas in the village has survived, and is worth visiting to see the lively carvings of mythical beasts on the capitals of the doorway. During July and August there is a *son-et-lumière* at the church.

Eleanor of Aquitaine was born at Nieul-sur-l'Autise not far from Maillezais in 1122. Her fateful marriage to Henry II of England after her divorce from Louis VII of France brought most of south-west France under English rule and was to lead eventually to the Hundred Years War (see p.48). Her birthplace is now marked by the former abbey of Saint-Vincent, which was restored in the last century. It is curious to think that the graceful cloister here was a new building when she was born.

The next leg of the tour is to Olbreuse, 45 km south across the marshes. From Maillezais, travel on the D15 and D116 through the web of canals and over the Sèvre to Courçon, and then through the northern edge of the Forêt de Benon to Mauzé-sur-le-Mignon, where you take the D101 to Olbreuse. Although this is quite a long way, the going is very easy. It is worth stopping at Mauzé, or returning to it, to see the renaissance château and the 12th-century church of Saint-Pierre. The famous French explorer René Caille, who was the first European to reach Timbuktu on the edge of the Sahara in the 1820s, was born in the village.

At Olbreuse you can stay in the old château which has been lived in by the Desmier family since 1335. It was restored in the 1970s and M. and Mme Arrive, members of the original family, turned it into a small hotel in 1983. The historic atmosphere of the Château d'Olbreuse is reflected in the four-poster beds, where you are awakened in the morning by the sound of cockerels crowing. The old kitchen is a small museum and the stable has been converted into a restaurant.

Visit Surgères from here, 12 km away on the D911, where a tower, some crumbling walls and a moat are all that remain of the castle. The church of Notre-Dame, which dates from the 1100s, has an exuberantly carved façade and an octagonal bell-tower.

The next halt is Villiers-en-Bois, where the tiny Auberge des Cedres is another rural establishment set in the middle of green fields and beautiful woodland. The hotel has only five rooms, but its restaurant is busy, particularly at weekends, and a warm welcome is guaranteed. Take the D109 east for 10 km from Olbreuse to Prissé-la-Charrière and then continue along the D53 for 7 km. The last part of the ride takes you through the overhanging greenery of the Forêt de Chizé, which became a royal forest in 1350. You can still glimpse deer through the trees here. Just outside the village is the European Zoorama, a large and delightful woodland zoo in which some 600 animals, including bison, goats, deer, boar, wild cats, lizards and snakes, live in a natural environment. There is a butterfly museum nearby.

Aulnay to the south, 20 km away on the D1 and D950, was another stopping-place for pilgrims en route to Santiago de Compostela in northern Spain. Its huge romanesque church of Saint-Pierre-de-la-Tour, built in the 1100s, is surrounded by an ancient cemetery. The carvings on the capitals in the church are very fine, as is the lively detail over the arches of the doorway.

From Villiers-en-Bois the next halt, Celles-sur-Belle (see p.85), is 22 km to the north, along the D119 and D103. From there, it is only another 19 km to the starting-point of Saint-Maixent-l'Ecole and to the end of a tour of what is surely one of the calmest and most calming places left in Europe, a land of green silences.

CHAPTER FOUR

COGNAC
AND THE
DORDOGNE

'ANYTHING MAY HAPPEN IN FRANCE,' said François, Duc de la Rochefoucauld, an ornament of the court of Louis XIV and one of the great observers of the human condition. Anyone who has had the pleasure of cycling in rural France will know the truth of his remark, especially perhaps those who explore this part of the country, which has so many secret and unexpected corners.

One minute you may be cycling along quietly, the next plunged into one of those unexpected incidents that you will be able to talk about for months afterwards. One couple suddenly found themselves in the middle of a parade at a village festival at Mareuil-sur-Belle. Everyone was in 19th-century costume, the village girls in long skirts and bonnets riding on huge horse-drawn farm carts and gendarmes on horseback waving their swords to keep order.

Other friends always planned a day's outing so they could picnic by one of the many streams and rivers, usually crossing by one bridge and coming back by another, so that they could return to their hotel by a different route. One day, though, the plan misfired and an expected bridge did not materialize. Fortunately a punt appeared around a bend in the river, with an

old man at the pole and his granddaughter playing the mouth-organ. At once he ferried the cyclists across the stream.

Another couple cycled into Bourdeilles to find the streets decked with bunting and crowds of people lining the main road in carnival mood. Police arrived, waving flags and blowing whistles. But before the couple could dismount, some 30 cyclists zoomed past at high speed. They followed on slowly up the steep hill to the centre of town to loud cheers from the crowds, who had gathered to witness the local cycle race, three hours of high-speed pedalling in a temperature of 26°C.

A good starting-point for touring this region is la Rochefoucauld, where the duke, the sixth of his line, had his château. His *Maxims*, first published in 1665, have gained him immortality with their pithy reflections. Among other jewels, it was he who noted that 'we have all enough strength to bear other people's troubles' and that 'hypocrisy is the homage paid by vice to virtue'.

La Rochefoucauld the place is less daunting than the person. It is a delightful small town, busy with local commerce, overlooked by the family's magnificent château and surrounded by beautiful countryside. The Poitou-Charente region in which it lies stretches from Bourdeaux to Poitiers and was once part of Aquitaine, the territory that England and France were to dispute for so long during the 1300s. The landscape is varied, with often superb scenery. The region is centred on the river Charente, which winds lazily north, then south, before turning west to make its languid way to the Atlantic. Rolling farmland gives way to woodland and vine-covered hillsides. Around Cognac to the west the vineyards stretch into the distance, growing the grapes that will be transformed into golden brandy. Narrow, winding roads follow meandering streams edged with poplars and wil-lows. Villages and hamlets stud the landscape, while from time to time glowering châteaux recall earlier, less peaceful times.

Cycling here is mostly easy, with only gentle climbs over the low ridges that separate river valleys. The landscape becomes gradually hillier towards the east, and if you venture far into the Dordogne you will be faced with some steep ascents. The climate is mild, with warm springs that arrive early in the year. During the summer, though, it can be very hot. Autumn is perhaps the most enchanting season, when it is still warm and heather adds a bloom of purple to the hills. Be prepared for some wet days—although it is an inland area, winds from the Atlantic can bring rain all year round.

The château at la Rochefoucauld is set on a hill (*la Roche*) overlooking the river Tardoire and was originally known as la Roche-à-Foucauld. It dates from the Middle Ages, with new wings and towers being added over the centuries, and is still owned by the family. During the night of 28 January 1960 a large part of the keep collapsed, the foundations having been undermined by the river. Each summer, during July, there is a *son-et-lumière* at the château and you can visit the gardens and the interior, with its renaissance staircase, throughout the year. Other attractions in the town include cloisters dating from the 1400s which can still be seen at a former Carmelite convent now used as a school. The church of Saint-Cybard, with its gothic architecture, is also well worth a visit.

The town is not famous for its wine, but the local co-operative is none the less very successful, and provides many hotels in the area with their house wines. The place where I like to stay is La Vieille Auberge, a small country inn situated in a quiet street a few hundred metres from the centre of town.

South-west of la Rochefoucauld, 20 km away down the N141, is Angoulême, the largest town of the region and well worth an excursion. This ancient, fortified city standing above the river Charente was already well established in Roman times and still has many old buildings. The cathedral of Saint-Pierre, built in the

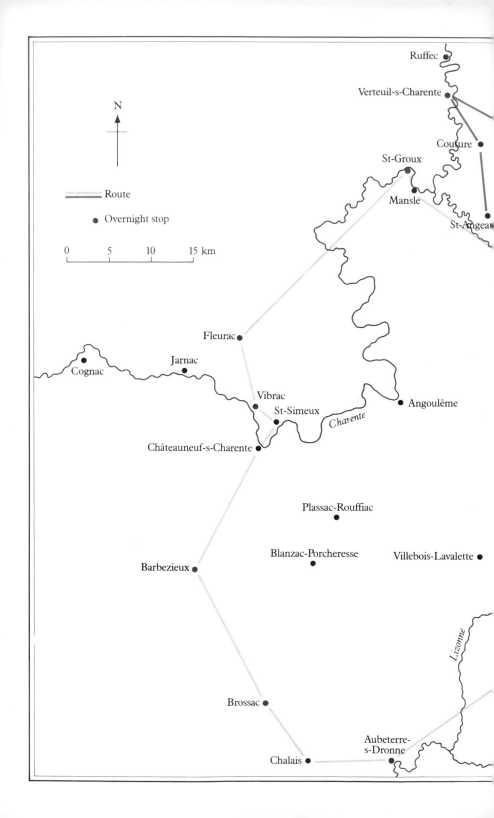

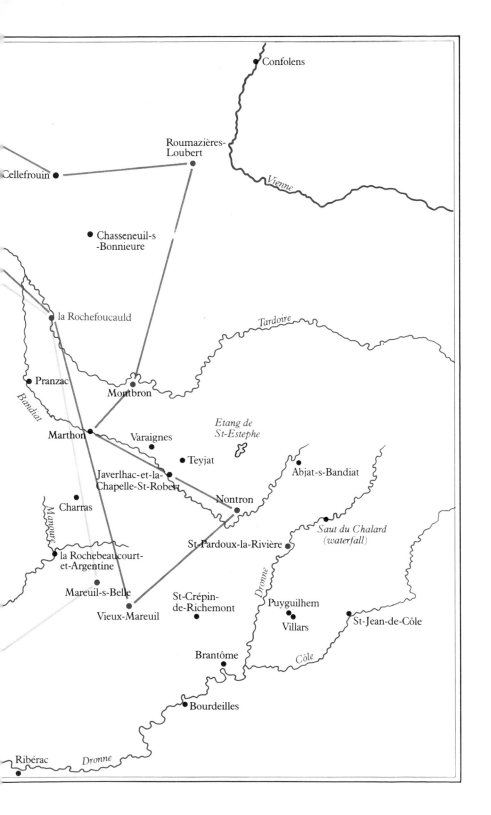

1100s, is quite magnificent, with a carved façade depicting the Last Judgement. You can see beautiful houses dating from the 1500s in the surrounding streets.

Another outing from la Rochefoucauld would be to visit Chasseneuil, 8 km to the north-east along the N141. There is a memorial to members of the French Resistance here and an interesting old church.

A week's gentle touring from la Rochefoucauld could take you north to Verteuil and Roumazières-Loubert, and then south to Montbron, Nontron and Mareuil. A fortnight of slightly harder riding would enable you to make a circuit of the area, travelling from la Rochefoucauld to Mareuil, Aubeterre, Brossac, Barbezieux, Vibrac, Fleurac and Saint-Groux.

Verteuil is 32 km north of la Rochefoucauld. Take the D6 to Saint-Angeau and then the D15 and D26 through Couture, where the interior of the church dates from the 1100s. A few kilometres further on the D26 you will see Verteuil, with its magnificent 14th-century château standing high over the bank of the river Charente. Unfortunately, this spectacular building is not open to the public. The village also has a 12th-century church and an ancient convent. Look for the signs to the Hôtel la Paloma, which is about 1 km away. This tiny *auberge* surrounded by fields and chickens and friendly goats is one of the most relaxing I know. When the weather is warm you can sip your aperitif outside, before eating a delicious supper in the rustic restaurant.

While at Verteuil visit Ruffec just to the north on the D26. This is a charming village with narrow streets of ancient houses mouldering in the sunshine and the old church of Saint-André.

To reach Roumazières you cycle to the south-east for 30 km through some lovely countryside and charming little villages. Take the D26, turning on to the D739 through Cellefrouin, which has an abbey church dating from the 11th century. Then continue on the D739 and D172, turning left to Roumazières, a pleasant small town which has three churches dating from the 12th century. The Hôtel du Commerce is set in a restful garden away from busy roads. (I have found that hotels with the word *commerce* in their titles are generally good value.) You eat in a dining-room with a rustic atmosphere, with a quarry-tiled floor and beamed ceiling. The food is excellent and specialities include *escargots à la charentaise* and *tournedos périgourdin*. Market day in the village is on Sunday.

There is a very pretty ride 14 km north from here along the banks of the Vienne to Confolens. This small town is famous for its folk festival in August when the narrow streets are crowded with dancers and musicians, brightly dressed in national costumes from all over the world. At other times of the year Confolens is much quieter and you can stroll peacefully through its medieval streets.

From Roumazières, you could cycle directly south to Montbron, following the D16 most of the way. Montbron is set in the beautiful valley of the river Tardoire and has a château dating from the 1400s and a church built in the 1200s. I think you will be surprised by the Hôtel des Trois Marchands in the town square. It looks like a little café with a busy restaurant; but at the back there are modern, elegant bedrooms. You can swim in the local pool and there is a big market in the town for three days in early July. From here you could visit the Grottes du Quéroy, off the D699 to the west, to see the stalactite formations in the caves. You will pass through Pranzac on the Bandiat on the way, where there is a renaissance church and a *lanterne-des-morts*, where corpses would rest overnight before burial.

The next stop is at Nontron, a small town perched on a promontory that lies between the valley of the river Bandiat and a deep ravine. You could cycle there by way of Marthon, 8 km south-west of Montbron on the D16, where there is a ruined château by the river Bandiat. I am surprised Nontron is still there. It has been conquered by the Romans and the Goths and laid waste by the Saracens. In the 840s, the Normans slaughtered every man they found after a long siege. It still retains traces of its original fortifications, although the charming château, built in the 1700s, has replaced a grimmer castle. Surprisingly it is now an antique doll museum.

It is worth climbing up to the large terrace with the war memorial near the château for a spectacular view over the town clinging to the sides of the ravine below. The countryside around is wild and rocky and some of the outcrops have weathered into strange, seemingly distorted shapes. There are markets on Wednesday and Saturday. The Grand Hôtel where I recommend staying is in the centre of the town. Take the top road through Nontron as otherwise you will find yourself going down the hill, only to have to climb back up the other side. The hotel has been in the same family for several generations and is now run by the three Pélisson brothers and their wives. It features an excellent restaurant serving Périgordien food.

A good day trip from here would be to cycle some 18 km east to see the Saut du Chalard waterfall, where the river Dronne foams down over rocks in a narrow ravine. On the way there you can visit Saint-Pardoux-la-Rivière on the D83, which has a ruined convent dating from the 1200s.

North of Nontron is the calm lake of Saint-Estephe where you can swim or go canoeing. Take the D675 for 8 km, and then turn left. A little beyond the lake there is a series of small waterfalls, formed where the stream gushes and rushes through woodland over a rocky bed. Make a round trip through the town of Abjat-sur-Bandiat to the east. There are two châteaux here, the medieval Château de la Malignie and the Château Balleran, dating from the 1500s. There is also an interesting church, which was built in the 1200s and restored 400 years later.

Alternatively, go west from the lake of Saint-Estephe to Teyjat, where the Grotte de la Mairie is a cave that was inhabited by prehistoric man. On the walls are drawings of deer and horses made around 30,000 years ago. From here you could join the D75 and go west to Varaignes, where the château dating from the 1400s is now a folk museum. A feast is held in the courtyard here on the first Sunday in August every year as part of an annual fair. The sweet-toothed will be pleased to discover that macaroons and meringues are a local speciality. Returning down the D75 to Nontron, you could visit Javerlhac-et-la-Chapelle-Saint-Robert, named after the 13th-century abbey church nearby. The Château de Javerlhac is a massive building with a great round tower.

Vieux-Mareuil is only a short ride from Nontron by the direct route down the D708 and D93. Much more enjoyable, however, is to take the time to make a detour east to visit Puyguilhem, Brantôme and places nearby, although only the very energetic would want to do the total distance suggested—about 70 km— in a day. Puyguilhem south-east of Nontron on the D3 has a splendid château, completed in the 1530s and restored to its former glory in the 1950s. It is a renaissance building of great beauty with a massive circular tower and a polygonal staircase. The village of Villars nearby has charming old houses and a 16th-century church, while there are prehistoric paintings and bizarre rock formations in the Grottes de Villars on the D82 to the north. You can also see the ruins of Boschaud abbey just outside Villars, founded by Cistercian monks in 1154 close by one of the pilgrimage routes to Compostela in Spain. Although the abbey was devastated in the Hundred Years War, the ruins are well preserved, perhaps because the site is so isolated. Go on a few kilometres east to Saint-Jean-de-Côle, on the D707, a medieval village that typifies the region at its best. Old houses, an ancient humpback bridge across the river Côle and its rounded romanesque church dating from the 1100s give it an ageless charm. The Château de la Marthonie has 14th-century towers, although most of it dates from a century or two later. It can be visited during July and August.

From Saint-Jean, cycle down the D78 along the river Côle to Brantôme, an exquisite riverside town backed up against cliffs bordering the Dronne. It has a magnificent abbey, now deconsecrated, which was founded by the great emperor Charlemagne in the 780s. He presented it with the body of one of the children killed by King Herod, although it is not clear where he obtained this holy relic. An unusual dog-leg hump-back bridge by the abbey turns a corner as it crosses the river. Behind the abbey, you can see some impressive bas-reliefs of the crucifixion and the Last Judgement in caves in the cliff face. The town has several good restaurants and is something of a mecca for gourmets.

Bourdeilles, with its impressive castle on the river Dronne, is a little further south. The road running alongside the river is exceptionally pretty, with limestone cliffs on the other side, some of them honeycombed with caves which have been turned into dwellings in the past. Bourdeilles is completely dominated by its magnificent château, an imposing mass of ramparts and buildings. There is a wonderful view of the valley of the Dronne from the top of the medieval octagonal keep. The walls also enclose a renaissance château which was built in the mid 1500s to impress and accommodate the powerful Catherine de' Medici, then the Queen Mother of France, on a royal tour of the region, but she stayed elsewhere and it was never completed. Nevertheless the building has some impressive rooms, notably the Gold Room, which contains elaborate painted decorations. The château is now a museum specializing in French and Spanish furniture of the 16th and 17th centuries.

Between the castle walls and the nearby medieval bridge is an old ivy-covered mill with a stone prow shaped like a boat and water flowing by it on both sides. The castle was held by the English for a time in the early 1300s, before being retaken by Bertrand du Guesclin, one of France's great heroes of the Middle Ages. It was here, too, that Pierre de Bourdeilles, Seigneur de Brantôme, was born in 1540. Crippled by a fall from his horse after an active life as a soldier, he retired to the abbey of Brantôme and there wrote the scandalous memoirs that still provide a vivid portrait of his times. They were first published in 1659, some 45 years after his death at the age of 74. He is buried in the chapel of the Château de Richemont that he built 7 km from Brantôme. To see it, take the D939 north from Brantôme, turning right to Saint-Crépin-de-Richemont.

The places on this suggested route from Nontron can also be visited on excursions from the Auberge de l'Etang Bleu, 2 km out of Vieux-Mareuil, a little village well off the beaten track on the D93. As the hotel's name suggests, there is a blue lake in the park that surrounds it where you can swim. This purpose-built building is a comfortable place to stay, with elegant bedrooms and warm, stylish reception rooms. The park also has a little train which carries passengers. Vieux-Mareuil itself has a fortified church dating from the 1200s with three domes. La Roche-foucauld is a day's ride north from here.

Mareuil-sur-Belle to the west of Vieux-Mareuil is the first stop on a longer tour from la Rochefoucauld. This pleasant little village on the banks of the river Belle was once a flourishing fishing port. The Auberge du Moulin Fontverte here is a very small hotel—it has three bedrooms—converted from a derelict watermill. The old machinery has been used imaginatively as decoration around the hotel and the mill-stream runs under the restaurant, where the cuisine includes many local specialities, such as dishes containing walnuts and rice. The village has a small romanesque church, Saint-Paradoux, with a dome and a beautiful bell-tower, as well as another dating from the 1100s. The château of Mareuil was the seat of one of the four baronies of Périgord, but nothing remains of the original building where the troubadour Arnaud de Mareuil was born in 1150. The château seen today dates from the 15th and 16th centuries. Two impressive towers guard the splendid gatehouse and the bridge over a moat that no longer exists. There are underground dungeons in the château and a remarkable gothic chapel, a gem of Flamboyant architecture. There are several other châteaux in the area which are worth visiting. Those at Beaulieu and Beauregard are just south of Mareuil on the D708. The Château de Beauregard is lovely, with two square 14th-century towers and a range added in the 17th century. Look out for the attractive dovecote nearby. The Château le Repine to the south-east of Mareuil can be seen from the *Grande Randonnée 36*, part of the excellent network of tracks and paths which crosses France.

A rather longer excursion would take you to la Rochebeaucourt-et-Argentine, some 10 km north-west of Mareuil along the D939, where the rivers Lizonne and Manoure meet. There is a church dating from the 1200s here. Then take the D5 west for 8 km and you come to Villebois-Lavalette, a fortified hilltop village that was built some 700 years ago. Or go some 15 km north to Charras along the D939 and D25, where there is a 12th-century fortified church and a 17th-century château.

From Mareuil, you go south to Aubeterre-sur-Dronne (by the D708, D100 and D78), an ancient village set deep in the countryside overlooking a small river. It takes its name, literally 'white earth', from the chalk cliffs on which it stands. You can stay in the Hôtel du Périgord in the valley next to the river here or in the Auberge du Château in the village itself above the river. There are two interesting churches worth visiting: the monolithic church of Saint-Jean, which was carved out of the

COGNAC AND THE DORDOGNE

solid rock in the 1100s, and the romanesque church of Saint-Jacques, which was once a Benedictine abbey. You can swim in the local pool.

Ribérac a few kilometres upstream is worth an excursion. It is a pleasant country town of 4000 or so inhabitants, including quite a few expatriate Britons. Although this is an ancient town, there are few reminders of its historic past, apart from a heavily restored 12th-century church. There is also a Gallo-Roman tower on the other side of the Dronne that now forms part of the Château de la Rigale. During the autumn and early winter, from October to December, there is a weekly walnut market in the town on Wednesdays, while local basket-weavers hold a market on the same day in the summer. There is also a Friday market and fairs on the first Friday of the month from July to October.

The now vanished château at Ribérac was the birthplace of Arnaut Daniel, a troubadour who was noted for his technical skills and admired by later poets, including Dante and Petrarch. Daniel became a member of Richard the Lionheart's court, where he gained a reputation for writing the most eloquent love poetry of his time.

From Aubeterre take the D2 for 11 km to Chalais, an ancient hillside village that contains the remains of a Gallo-Roman forge. Its château, built in the 1500s, has three massive towers. Brossac, the next stop on the tour, is a village with a 12th-century church, some 11 km to the north-west of Chalais along the D731. There the Chambres d'Hôte is a delightful house that has been turned into a hotel. There are good bedrooms with en suite bathrooms but there is no restaurant. To eat, try the Hôtel du Commerce in the village.

From Brossac to Barbezieux, a town famous for its *marrons glacés*, is a ride of 20 km north along the D731. Barbezieux is another ancient place of narrow twisting streets and old houses. Its château, a building of the 1200s, has recently been restored.

In the centre of the town is the Hôtel la Boule d'Or, which has had the same owners for more than 25 years. Its reception area and restaurant are decorated in a delightful old-world style.

For a day's outing from here, take the D5 for 16 km to Blanzac-Porcheresse, where there is the château that was the ancient stronghold of the la Rochefoucauld family. There are also two interesting churches—Saint-Arthemy, which dates from the 1100s, and the domed church of Saint-Cybard de Porcheresse, built a century earlier. About 2 km further on, turn left on to the D436 to Plassac-Rouffiac, where there is a romanesque 12th-century church. The doorway of this delightful stone building with a small spire is set in three tiers of arches.

On the way from Barbezieux to Vibrac, 22 km to the north along the D14 and D22, you will pass Châteauneuf-sur-Charente, which has an interesting church. A detour from here by way of the scenic D84 would take you through Saint-Simeux, with its old water-mill. Vibrac is another small village set in a stretch of idyllic countryside, with the usual château and some 12th-century buildings. You will need to follow the signs to find the Hôtel les Ombrages, a lovely little hotel with its own swimming-pool and tennis court. Jarnac, 10 km to the north-west, is a pleasant town to visit from here and you could see it on the way to the tiny village of Fleurac. The Château de Fleurac, which dates from the 14th century, was restored about a hundred years ago and is now a hotel. The interior is delightful and the house is surrounded by a large garden.

Around Fleurac vineyards stretch away in all directions, an indication that you are now on the edge of Cognac country. This noble drink derives from an experiment with what amounted to a very inferior wine in the 1600s. The wine, a light, dry white, is heated in a copper cauldron until it boils and the alcohol is transformed into a vapour that passes down a swan's neck tube into a condenser. The following day it is reheated slowly to produce a potent liquid which is then aged in casks made of oak. It takes around 9 litres of wine to produce one of cognac— literally 'burnt wine'. The brandy's familiar amber colour comes from absorbing the tannin from the wood. Nowadays you can visit the distilleries of Hennessy, Hine and Martell—all firms founded by the English or the Irish—and see the process by which the wine is transformed into the best of brandy. The firm of Hennessy, for instance, was started by an Irishman who served with the French army and began in the 1760s by shipping brandy back to his homeland for his relatives to enjoy.

The locals drink a by-product of the production of cognac, an aperitif called Pineau. It comes in both a red form, which I find too sweet, and a white. The town of Cognac itself, a day's outing from Fleurac, has given its name to the best known of brandies. This is made from distilled wine which is then matured in casks of oak cut from the forests of Limousin, which give it its colour.

Cognac is a busy little town on the river Charente, but still retains many buildings from its medieval past. One of the old gateways into the town—the Porte Saint-Jacques—still stands by the river. Built in the 1500s, it has two squat round towers guarding a narrow entrance. The church of Saint-Léger, which dates from the 1100s, is still surrounded by old houses. You can also see the château where King François I was born in 1494, although it is no longer a royal palace. One interesting feature of the place is that many of the buildings in and around Cognac are blackened by a fungus that feeds on the alcohol which evaporates from the wooden brandy casks.

Saint-Groux, a country village on the banks of the Charente, lies 30 km to the north-east of Fleurac. You will need to follow the signs to discover the Hôtel les Trois Saules near the river. South for 3 km on the D361 from here is Mansle, another pleasing riverside town with its towering Château de Goue, built in the 1400s and improved in the 1700s when fortresses went out of fashion. It seems an appropriate place to end a visit to the region, for it encapsulates the charm of the area: the slow-moving river, the green countryside, the ancient buildings suggestive both of war and pleasure and the intimate scale of the landscape round about. La Rochefoucauld is a short ride south-east on the D6.

CHAPTER FIVE

BORDEAUX
AND
GARONNE

CROSSED BY THREE GREAT RIVERS—the Lot, Garonne and Dordogne—this is a deeply rural area of France. The countryside watered by these rivers is rich and fertile, growing everything from asparagus and melons to lusciously plump tomatoes. The scale of the area is small and intimate, and the landscape is immensely variable. One minute you are cycling past fields of vegetables, or rolling hills covered in corn, the next you are plunged into woodland, or into the orchards which have given this region its nickname of 'little California'. The warm sun that ripens the famous Bordeaux grapes also helps produce an enormous variety of fruit: apples, cherries, peaches, pears, plums and nectarines among them. Soft fruit grows in abundance and is often for sale along the roadside.

The regional cuisine reflects the produce of this rich area of France. Local farmers fatten their geese and ducks to produce *pâté de foie gras* and the delicacy known as *confit*, in which delectable chunks of poultry are cooked and preserved in their own fat. Fried *confit* is present on most menus. But the great gastronomic glory of the region is the famous truffle, which grows underground and is usually collected with the help of a dog or pig, both of which have noses that are keen enough to detect the faint aroma of these elusive fungi. *Cèpes*, the huge wild mushrooms that grow throughout the region, are also delicious, particularly in omelettes, and many consider them a greater delicacy than truffles. If you eat steak or kidneys you are likely to have them served *à la bordelaise* in a sauce made with shallots and Bordeaux wine. Among the many fish to be found in the rivers, and on menus, the locals prize lampreys, a sort of eel that is caught in the spring and usually cooked in its own blood and wine.

The varied cuisine is matched by a wide range of local wines. The light, translucent red wines of Bordeaux, which the English have always called claret (a corruption of the French word *clairet*,

meaning clear) are produced in a small area around the city of the
same name which is some 20 or 30 km west of the region
covered here. But the vineyards stretch much further, producing
less famous but often delicious and inexpensive wines; my
favourite is Buzet, from the vines around Nérac, but other
varieties worth sampling are Côte de Duras, Marmandes and
Bruilhos, not to mention the delightful Bergeracs.

The English taste for the wines of Bordeaux dates from the
1150s, when Henry II married Eleanor of Aquitaine (see p.48). A
legacy of this period of English rule is that many of the
vineyards in the area still bear English names, such as Talbot,
Brown, Palmer and Boyd. Every autumn for 300 years a fleet
would carry the wines back to England. Many superb white
wines are also produced in this part of France, from Graves and
Entre-deux-Mers to the sweet Sauternes and Barsac that make
such a splendid accompaniment to fruit or puddings (although
the French insist that they are best drunk with the pâté that is a
speciality of Périgord).

The pleasant rolling countryside is made-to-measure for
none-too-strenuous biking through rich farmland and extensive
forests that are home to all kinds of wildlife. The climate is mild,
with summers that are often very hot. Early morning mists are
soon dispelled by the rising sun. If you can, come here in the
spring, when the fruit trees are in blossom, or in the autumn,
when the grapes have ripened on the vines. July and August are
best avoided.

A particular delight of this part of France are the so-called
'new towns', in fact built some seven centuries ago. Known as
bastides, these fortified towns were sponsored by both the
Plantagenet and the French kings in an attempt to define their
territories and defend their boundaries, but they helped the
English in particular to consolidate their grip on the Dordogne.
Between the Dordogne and the Garonne there are still 17

bastides built by the French and 12 founded by the English. Many of these extraordinary examples of medieval town planning still retain their outer walls and some, such as Monpazier, are nearly complete.

For over a century the frontier of the large territory of Aquitaine under the overlordship of the English kings swayed back and forth across south-west France. Then in 1337 Edward III claimed the French throne through his mother Isabella of France, thus ushering in the Hundred Years War. At first it seemed as if England would be successful, with the famous English victories at Crécy (1346), when English longbowmen triumphed over the heavily-armoured French knights, and later at Poitiers (1356), when Edward the Black Prince took King John of France captive, but earlier triumphs were later reversed. The dispute continued intermittently until 1453 when Joan of Arc won the battle of Castillon and the gallant John Talbot, Earl of Shrewsbury and leader of the English forces, was axed to death. England had lost all territory in France except Calais.

I begin my tours at Villeréal, about midway between the Dordogne and the Lot. The old town was one of the *bastides* built in the 1260s as part of the French defences, although it was held by the English during the Hundred Years War. All *bastides* were based on a simple geometric design, with streets laid out on a grid pattern. Narrow alleys between the houses acted as fire breaks, a necessary precaution in a town that was likely to be attacked or besieged. In the centre was a square which usually contained a covered market. The church stood nearby. The town was surrounded by walls punctuated with towers and pierced by fortified gateways. In Villeréal, many of the houses retain their medieval character and you can still trace the layout of the original town. At its heart the fortified church, with two towers, and the oak-pillared market still survive. I stay on the edge of town in the Hostellerie du Lac, which is set in a large park beside

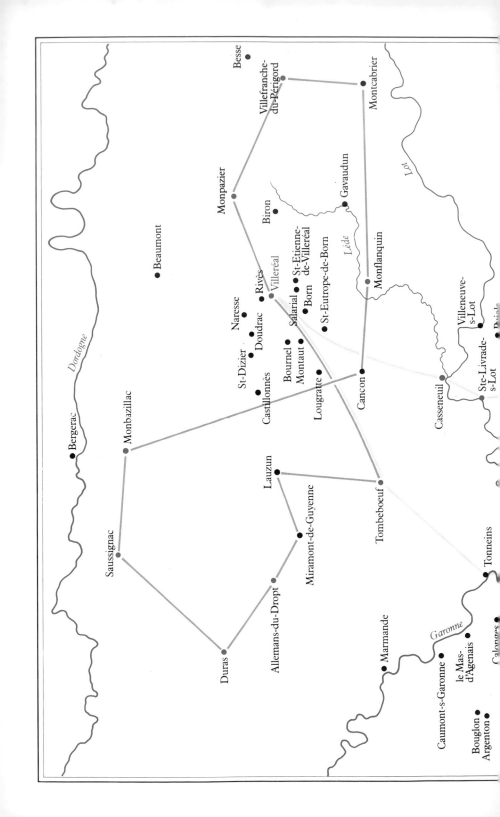

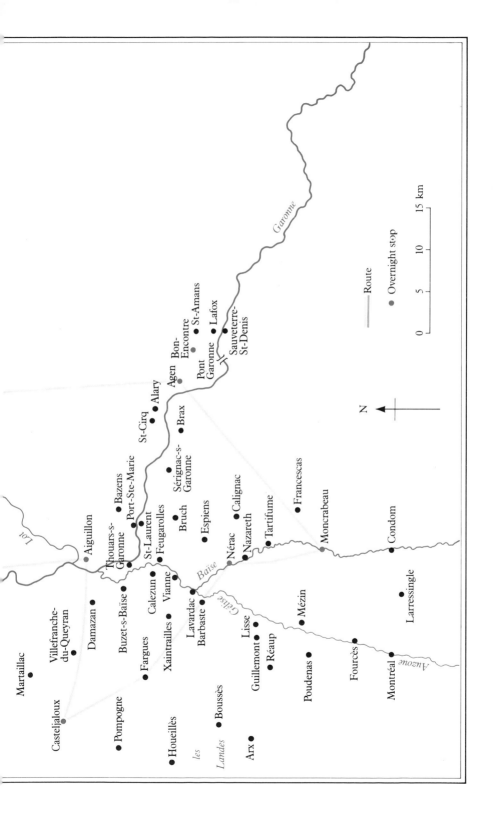

a trotting track used by horses and salukis. It has its own swimming-pool, although you can also swim in the nearby Lac de Pasquie.

There are several other *bastides* within a 30 km radius of the town, including Monflanquin and Villeneuve-sur-Lot to the south, Castillonnès to the west and Monpazier and Beaumont to the north, all built within 30 years of each other from 1255 onwards. A few days based in Villeréal touring these extraordinary towns would fascinate anyone interested in the Middle Ages and particularly in what Barbara Tuchman called 'the calamitous 14th century'. Her book *A Distant Mirror*, from which this quote comes, is the classic account of France at the time of the Black Death and the Hundred Years War.

Monpazier is 16 km to the north-east of Villeréal, along the D104 and D2. The most perfectly preserved of the *bastides*, it was built by Edward I of England, although it suffered at the hands of both sides in the Hundred Years War and also later, during the religious uprisings of the 16th century. Its walls still stand, as do three of its gateways, and the town's rectangular street pattern survives. Like those in Villeréal, each house is slightly separated from its neighbour to limit the effect of fire. Monpazier still has a wooden-roofed market, with covered arcades surrounding it. The leader of a peasant rebellion in the 1630s was executed here, by being broken on a wheel. The church and the chapter-house nearby both date from the foundation of the town, but the church has been much restored.

The Hôtel de France where we like to stay is in the Rue Saint-Jacques, one of the principal streets of the original *bastide*. It has a splendid 15th-century staircase and once had Lawrence of Arabia as a guest. Regional specialities—*cèpes, pâté de foie gras* and trout—are a feature here.

Overlooking the town from a vantage point 8 km away to the south (reached by the scenic D53) is the Château de Biron. This is one of the largest châteaux in the region and an awesome sight however you approach it. Built on a hilltop, the huge rambling complex of buildings is part medieval, part renaissance. The château's kitchens seem large enough to feed the entire population of the area. From its tower there are excellent views over Monpazier and the countryside around, almost as uninterrupted now as they were in the days when the castle's garrison watched anxiously for the approach of enemies. Of great strategic importance, Biron was much fought over in the Middle Ages. The village clustered round it only existed to serve the castle and several of the houses are huddled within its walls.

From Monpazier go north-west on the D660 for 16 km to Beaumont, another English *bastide*, although most of its fortifications have gone. The church of Saint-Front was built in the 1270s as much for defence as for worship, although restoration has disguised its might. Turn right on to the D25 for a further 12 km and you will be tracing the route once taken by many pilgrims to the abbey of Cadouin, which dates from the early 1100s. It was once a rich Cistercian monastery that owed its early prosperity to the possession of a linen cloth which had been brought from Antioch and was said to have been wrapped around the head of Christ on the cross. Richard the Lionheart was among those who came to venerate it. During the Hundred Years War, the relic was transferred to Toulouse in case it fell into English hands and was only regained for Cadouin with difficulty. Unfortunately the cloth was shown to experts in the 1930s who pronounced it to have been woven in the 10th century. The pilgrim trade collapsed, but the magnificent abbey, the finest in the Dordogne, still remains. The church itself is massive and simple, built of honey-coloured stone. The cloisters were begun in 1468 but were not completed for a hundred years, and are more richly decorated than the church.

Monflanquin lies 13 km directly south of Villeréal along the

D676. A hilltop *bastide* built by the French, it has a fortified church and the main square, the Place des Arcades, is surrounded by covered arcades. Just outside the town, on the road to Cancon, is the Moulin de Boulède, a good place to stay. The mill was converted to a hotel in the 1970s and has a garden running down to the river which once powered the mill wheel. Every Sunday lunchtime in summer the restaurant bursts its seams and spreads on to tables outside.

Travel 13 km to the east and you come to the tiny village of Gavaudun in the valley of the river Léde. A huge keep dating from the 1100s dominates the area from a rocky outcrop. Just beyond the village is the monastery of Saint-Sardos, where the Hundred Years War can be said to have begun. The first conflict was sparked off by ill-feeling between the local seigneur, who supported the English, and the pro-French monks. The baron attacked and slaughtered the community after they fortified the abbey, and it is now no more than a ruin.

Villeneuve-sur-Lot is 17 km south of Monflanquin along the D676. It was once one of the most powerful of the French *bastides*, but today only two of its fortified gateways still stand and the rest of the fortifications have disappeared as the town has expanded. The English built the Pont Vieux across the Lot in the late 1200s. Look out for the Musée de la Prune, which must be one of the few museums devoted to a fruit. This is an indication of the importance of plums in this region, the majority of which become prunes.

Just south of the town off the D118 is the ancient village of Pujols. Its stone fortifications standing above the valley of the Lot date back to the 1200s and there is a curious underground passage leading from the tower of Saint-Nicolas to the oldest part of the village.

Another ancient place worth visiting is Casseneuil (see p.124), 10 km north-west of Villeneuve on the river Lot, reached by the

D242 which runs beside the river. From there you can turn south for 7 km along the D217 to Sainte-Livrade-sur-Lot, a *bastide* that has long outgrown the area of the original walled settlement. This is now a thriving country town, particularly on Friday when the market draws business from a wide area in the valley of the Lot. But some reminders of its past history still remain, including the covered market, a tower, a church of the 1100s and a château The small Hôtel le Midi is an enjoyable place to stay here.

Some 8 km south, just off the D220, are the Grottes de Lestournelles. Carved out by streams over the centuries, these caves contain some interesting formations of stalactites and stalagmites.

Bastides will be found throughout the Dordogne, and there are also many other interesting places and glorious countryside to be seen. In an alternative tour from Villeréal, you could visit Monpazier, the lovely village of Villefranche further into the Dordogne, Montcabrier, Monflanquin and Monbazillac in a week's cycling. This route includes some minor hills, although you will find there is no road that requires strenuous effort. In ten days, you would have time to visit Saussignac, Duras, Allemans and Tombeboeuf as well.

To the south and west the going is gentler. In seven days from a base in Villeréal you would have time to explore Tombeboeuf, Aiguillon, Agen, Sainte-Livrade and Casseneuil. A further seven days would enable you to go even further west, visiting Casteljaloux, Nérac and Moncrabeau.

Whatever you plan, it is probably best not to try and push yourself too hard, although help is usually at hand if you do get stuck. A couple who had set off to explore the villages around Villeréal found that their enthusiasm had got the better of them. As darkness fell, they were still 17 km from the hotel, having cycled some 90 km. Wearily, they pushed their bikes up a hill and went to the local bar to see if anyone knew where they might find a taxi. There the owner came to their rescue. 'My son will drive you back,' she said, 'his father was English.' And he did.

The splendidly-preserved Monpazier is again the first stop on the tour around the northern half of the region. From there cycle 20 km east on the D660 to Villefranche-du-Périgord, where the covered market and arcaded main square of the original *bastide* still survive. The fountain in the square probably provided the inhabitants with fresh water during its many sieges. The Hôtel les Bruyeres often offers *périgordien* food, such as *foie gras* or *confit de canard*. One couple wrote to me to say that 'the spirit, good humour and enjoyment of the whole trip was summed up by an incident in Villefranche. We took the train to les Eyzies, got absolutely soaked to the skin and just managed to get our bikes back on an official "no bike carrying" train. Madame served us with a full meal although we were two hours late and the town had had no electricity all day. Her only comment was that it was *un peu bizarre* to drink port with coffee after a meal rather than as an aperitif.'

The countryside around Villefranche is delightful, with tiny, twisting lanes winding through luxuriant woods and picturesque stone hamlets. One of the most charming of these tiny settlements is Besse, 10 km north on the D57. Although it has fewer than 200 inhabitants, and is seemingly buried in a forest, there is a remarkable fortified church here, famous for the elaborate carvings on the west front, some of which date from the 11th century. The roof of the church is covered with stone slabs.

Montcabrier is 21 km south of Villefranche-du-Périgord. Take the D660 for 10 km to Frayssinet-le-Gélat and then turn right on to the D673. Montcabrier is a small village with fewer than 400 inhabitants and here too there is an interesting old church. Not far away is the massive Château de Bonaguil, well worth seeing although the route is a winding one. Continue along the D673 and turn right at Saint-Martin-le-Redon and then right again on to the D158.

Bonaguil is a monumental fortress. Built in the late 1400s, it was specially designed to withstand cannon fire. The much-hated Beranger de Roquefueil spent some 40 years fortifying it, at a time when most of his contemporaries were turning their castles into country mansions. It has thick outer walls; a huge barbican within; powerful, stolid towers and, as a final line of defence, a keep so devised that it presented a narrow profile to attackers. Beranger sunk a well down through the rock to provide fresh water for his garrison. The castle looks impregnable. We shall never know whether it was, since no one ever attacked it.

Monflanquin (see p.117) is 29 km west of Montcabrier by the D673 and the D124. From there it is 45 km to Monbazillac. Take the D124 west to Cancon (see p.123), turning right on to the N21 to Bouniagues. There, turn left and cycle through Ribagnac to Monbazillac, famous for the sweet wine produced from the vineyards here. The grapes are left to ripen and then rot on the vines until they are wrinkled and dried, when they are picked and pressed to make the golden Monbazillac. The château of Monbazillac stands amid the vineyards, which stretch away on all sides. It dates from the mid 1500s and is a stately mansion of grey walls and brown-tiled roofs, surrounded by a dry moat. There is a splendid great hall and a display of antique wine-making equipment in its cellars. Not far away—along the D14 and then left on the D107—is the Château de Bridoire, a similar building in an almost identical setting. It is not, however, open to the public.

Monbazillac also has a pleasant restaurant, but stay in the Relais de la Diligence just north of the village, overlooking the vineyards on the road from Bergerac. The panoramic views across the countryside from here are a bonus.

Across the Dordogne river, 6 km or so north of Monbazillac, is Bergerac, best known for its long-nosed lover, Cyrano de Bergerac, created by dramatist Edmond Rostand in 1897, and for its wines, including the red Pecharmont. Covering both banks of the Dordogne, it is an important agricultural centre. It also owes some of its prosperity to tobacco, which is grown in the area, and there is a museum devoted to the weed. This is housed in a 17th-century building that also includes a more general museum about the region.

With more time to spare, you could travel on from Monbazillac to Saussignac, which is 20 km to the west. The villages in this area often contain a château, a small hotel, a smattering of shops and a few houses, usually with magnificent vegetables growing in their gardens. The Relais de Saussignac is another hotel deep in the countryside, nicely off the beaten track.

Duras is south-west from here—take the D4 for 10 km to Margueron, turning left on to the D708. Clustered round its castle perched on a hilltop, the town overlooks vineyards and rolling farmland and is an important agricultural centre. Market day is on Monday and there are festivals during August and September. But the focus of interest is the Château des Ducs, which, according to local legend, was designed by an Englishman. It had eight massive towers and crenellated walls that surrounded an area 100 metres long by 30 metres wide. Its barons tended to side with the English in the Hundred Years War, and it was often besieged. It was gradually transformed into a country house and was then sacked during the French Revolution. The stone from seven of its towers was used to build locks on the nearby canal. Happily it is now being restored. This tumultuous history is best contemplated at the Hostellerie des Ducs, where you can eat well and drink the excellent local wine before retiring for the night.

Allemans-du-Dropt, a town with a well-settled air about it, is

17 km south-east of Duras along the D668. L'Etape Gascogne, where I like to stay, is a small hotel on the edge of the town. Wander into the local church to see the 15th-century frescoes. From here cycle east for 8 km along the D668 to Miramont (where you could refresh yourself in the town's swimming-pool) and then along the D1, and you come to Lauzun. The château here dates from the 1400s, although it was added to up until the 19th century. It once belonged to one of Louis XIV's favourites.

Directly south of Lauzun, reached by back roads or along the D667, is the village of Tombeboeuf, a ride of about 20 km. The Hôtel du Nord is also the village café and all the locals tend to drop in for a drink and a chat sometime during the day. There is a splendid view from the restaurant here. You can swim at Cancon, 17 km to the east along the D124. Another of the region's hilltop towns, Cancon is crowned by a ruined château and has houses dating from the 1500s leaning over narrow streets.

Tombeboeuf is also the first port of call on an exploration west from Villeréal. From there you head south to Aiguillon. The direct route is to follow the D120 for 19 km to Tonneins, then taking the N113 for 11 km. Aiguillon is in a beautiful position, overlooking the confluence of the Lot and the Garonne. The Château des Ducs there dates in parts from the 11th century. The recommended Hôtel les Cygnes is on the D666 on the way into town. It lives up to its name, with swans floating majestically on the pond in the garden. Not far from Aiguillon—6 km to the west on the D8—is Damazan, another well-preserved *bastide* that still has much of its ancient walls, towers and old houses.

A delightful ride east from here takes you along back roads to Bazens, where the ruined 15th-century château was once inhabited by the bishops of Agen. Among them was the Italian Matteo Bandello, who also wrote stories which Elizabethan playwrights, including Shakespeare, plundered for their plots. Next to the château is a restored church that is well worth a visit.

Further east from here along the N113 is Agen, a market town famed for its prunes and its rugby team. It is a pleasant place of 30,000 or so inhabitants with a picturesque old centre. The Musée des Beaux-Arts, housed in some 16th-century mansions, has an interesting collection. It includes a Greek sculpture of Venus, dug up by a farmer in the last century, a sensitive self-portrait by Goya and one of the finest paintings by the 19th-century French landscape painter Jean Corot, as well as a number of Impressionist works. Saint-Caprais's cathedral dates from the 11th century. Here again I like to stay on the outskirts of town in the Hostellerie de la Rigalette, set in a delightful garden. To find it take the N113 towards Aiguillon and then the D302. Alternatively, take the N113 south towards Toulouse for 2 km to Bon-Encontre, where the Hôtel le Parc is a delightful little stone building set at the end of a small public park, although it does not have its own restaurant.

From Agen it is 30 km to Sainte-Livrade-sur-Lot (see p.119). Take the N21 north and call in on the way at the Grottes de Fontirou at Castella, though it is a stiff climb to these interesting caves. Just beyond Sainte-Livrade, 6 km away on the D217, is Casseneuil, a pleasant village lying between the rivers Lot and Léde. Its church dates from the 1100s and has decorative friezes in the nave. The Auberge la Résidence here is an attractive small hotel.

Villeréal is now a day's journey away. Those with more time could extend the tour by travelling further west from Aiguillon, first visiting Casteljaloux, a 25 km ride along the D8 and D11. This bustling town is on the edge of the country known as *les Landes*, with its extensive pine forests and sandy beaches along the Atlantic coast. Shepherds here are said to walk on stilts to keep them above the rough and treacherous ground. The town's market day is Saturday and you can swim in the nearby lake as well as a swimming-pool. Casteljaloux has a well-preserved medieval quarter and during the summer months everywhere is decorated with flowers. The hospitable Hôtel aux Cadets de Gascogne is a typical French provincial hotel with the added bonus of a garden where you can breakfast out of doors.

A fairly tough but rewarding ride is from Casteljaloux to Marmande and back, a distance of 70 km. Take the D252 from the town, turning right on to the D106 to Argenton. Stay on the D106 for a further 2 km to Bouglon, then taking the D147 for 3 km to Guérin, where you turn on to the C1 past le Bois, and then right on to the D116 to Marmande. This small town has suffered much destruction over the centuries, from the Visigoths and the Saracens to the French and the English during the Hundred Years War. Some fortifications remain on the banks of the Garonne and the church of Notre-Dame dates from the 1200s, though it was added to in the 1400s and 1600s. Marmande's restaurants include the Hôtel de Bretagne, near the station, and the Auberge du Guyenne.

From Marmande you make your way back towards Casteljaloux along the D933, turning left on to the D143 to Caumont, a distance of 10 km. Continue along the road for 5 km to le Mas-d'Agenais, with its wooden market-place and 12th-century church. From here you can take a short cut along the D6 by way of Martaillac to Casteljaloux, a distance of 17 km. Those with energy can stay on the D143 to see the 17th-century château at Calonges, continuing for 12 km along the C5 to the *bastide* of Damazan. If you feel a little hungry by this time, visit the Hôtel du Commerce in the town. Then take the D108 for 8 km to Villefranche-du-Queyran, and the D261 for 9 km to Casteljaloux.

The next stop is Nérac, 30 km to the south-east, along a road (the D655) through forest and farmland. A few kilometres before the town you come to Barbaste, on the eastern edge of the *Landes*, where prosperity was once based on harvesting the cork oaks of the forest. The fortified mill on the river Gélise is known as the Moulin d'Henri IV, and is said to have been one of the king's favourite haunts. Its four towers are all of different heights.

Henri is also associated with the Château de Nérac, which once had a reputation as a centre of courtly love, and which Shakespeare chose as the setting for *Love's Labours Lost*. Despite being not what it was in its heyday, the building still retains a romantic charm, although its furnishings are disappointing. Henri loved to walk in what is now the public park, shady with trees on the banks of the river. A statue next to a pool commemorates a peasant girl who drowned herself there after being seduced by the young Henri. Stay in the Hôtel d'Albret, particularly if you like melons, one of the local specialities, which are featured here. Or patronise the Hôtel du Château opposite the magnificent château in the centre of town. Market day is Saturday, and there is a swimming-pool if you feel like some alternative exercise.

Moncrabeau is 12 km south down the D930, a small village apparently miles from anywhere. The quiet roads, green fields and open vistas broken only by small villages and the occasional interesting building make this ideal cycling country. Once you leave the village, though, you will not find many shops so it is best to buy food for a picnic before you set out. You can swim in the local pool. The Hôtel le Phare here has great charm.

Two places worth visiting are a short cycle ride away. Mézin, 11 km to the west along the D219 and D117, has a 12th-century church and an Armagnac warehouse. Just beyond the village, 4 km further on, is Poudenas, where there is a château and an excellent restaurant.

From Moncrabeau it is an interesting cross-country ride to Agen, from where you could continue to follow the route of the shorter tour (see p.124). A different approach to cycling in the Dordogne is to explore one section of the region more intensively, by staying in one town and venturing out on different trips each day. Both Agen and Nérac are good centres for visiting areas off the beaten track.

There are also several enjoyable rides to be had around Villeréal itself, such as the following round trip of about 40 km. Take the D207 for 1 km to Rivès, where the church of Saint-Pierre is worth a look. A little further on, to the right, is the Château de Jouandous and, on the left, the Château de Fonrives which dates from the 1500s. Neither is open to the public. Go through the village of Naresse, take the first road to the left to Doudrac and then follow the D250 through the delightful valley of the Dropt towards Saint-Dizier. From there, make for Bournel to the south and then take the D218 to Montaut. You can see north across the valley of the Dropt from here and to the château of Biron to the east. Montaut itself has the remains of ancient fortifications, as well as medieval houses and a church with a 13th-century door. Then go west towards Lougratte and take the third road on the left to Saint-Eutrope, through the woods of Cluzélou. Go through the village and take the first road to the left to see the exterior of the Château de Séandaillac, which was begun in the 13th century, remodelled in the 16th, and restored from its ruinous state more recently.

Return to the road from Saint-Eutrope and continue towards Saint-Vivien. Then take the D153 north through Born, where you can glimpse a château dating from the 1200s. Turn left at the crossroads with the D676 and then take the first turning on the right for a charming ride through the tiny, crumbling villages of Salarial and Saint-Etienne to a shady, country road that takes you back to Villeréal.

Using Nérac as a base, you could spend several days exploring the country round about without exhausting all the delights of the neighbourhood. You might not see many famous sights, but you would get a magnificent taste of rural France, away from the familiar tourist haunts. Easy rides would take you to the fortified village of Larressingle, to the ancient town of Barbaste and the château at Buzet-sur-Baïse, or along the valley of the little river Baïse. More strenuous riding would take you to Agen, to Casteljaloux, or to Aiguillon.

To visit Larressingle, take the D930 for 21 km to Condom, then turn right on to the D15, taking a turning on the left after 5 km to Larressingle. Return to the D15 and continue for another 10 km to Montréal, where there is a restaurant for those who feel in need of a lunchtime break. From here, follow the course of the river Auzoue for 6 km to Fourcès. Then take the D5 north, turning on to the D656 to Mézin (see p.126), which will lead you 13 km back to Nérac.

A shorter round trip of 40 km would enable you to visit Buzet-sur-Baïse, which has a château dating from the 1400s, Calezun, with its 11th-century church, Vianne, where there are traces of medieval fortifications and Barbaste, with its fortified 14th-century mill and Roman bridge.

From Nérac, take the D136 towards Espiens, and continue west to Lavardac. From there turn right on to the D930 to Trenqueleon, which has a château of the 1600s. Then continue through Feugarolles to Thouars on the river Garonne. It is another 3 km along the D12 to Buzet-sur-Baïse, where it is well worth sampling the wine from the local vineyards—red, white and rosé are all enjoyable. You could combine a tasting with lunch at La Table Buzequaise. From here, take the D642 to Calezun and Vianne and on to Lavardac, where you turn right on to the D655 for the 2 km ride to Barbaste. From there you can return to Nérac by back roads along the river Baïse, cycling along the opposite bank to the one on which you started.

Another easy ride of 34 km would take you along the bank of the Baïse to Nazareth, with its interesting 13th-century church and ruined keep, and to Moncrabeau, which has a church of the same period. From Nérac, take the D656 towards Agen and then turn on to the C1 for Nazareth, a distance of 2 km. Now cycle along the D131 and then the D232 to Tartifume and Francescas, some 9 km in all. You could then make a detour of 3 km along the D112 to the château of Lasserre before returning to Francescas and heading south, turning right on to the C1 to Moncrabeau, a further 9 km. From there continue along the C1, turning right at the junction with the D930, which takes you the 12 km along the Baïse back to Nérac.

The ride to Agen, which is 28 km from Nérac on the D656, is harder. To add a little variety on the return trip, turn right on to the D119 after crossing the Garonne. This will take you through Brax, some 7 km from Agen, and Sérignac 6 km further on, which has an 11th-century church and a reasonable restaurant, Le Relais Landais. From Sérignac, turn left on to the D286 and then right on to the D656 which brings you back through Calignac to Nérac.

An even tougher ride is the 80 km trip to Casteljaloux, but this takes you through three villages with fortified churches—Houeillès, Pompogne and Fargues—as well as to a part medieval, part renaissance château at Lisse. The Restaurant des Landes at Houeillès and the Restaurant de la Gare at Casteljaloux provide opportunities for refreshment. From Nérac take the D656 towards Mézin, turning right after a few kilometres to Lisse, a total distance of 9 km. From here, there is delightful cycling along back roads to Guillemont and Réaup, a further 8 km. Then head for Arx, 12 km away to the west, turning right on to the D59 to Boussès, another 5 km, and keeping straight on on the D434 for the 8 km ride to Houeillès. From Houeillès, the D933 takes you the 6 km to Pompogne and a further 8 km to Casteljaloux (see p.124). On the return trip, follow the D655 through Fargues, a distance of 10 km, staying on the road for another 4 km to Placiot. Then turn left on to the D141 for a 5 km ride to Xaintrailles, where there is a 15th-century château which was the home of one of Joan of Arc's supporters. According to local legend a princess who lived there was turned into a snake for one day a week as punishment for killing her father. She is said to haunt the place still. Then take the D108 to Lavardac and the D930 back to Nérac.

The round trip to Aiguillon covers about 50 km and is also a moderately hard ride. You pass through Espiens, which has a keep dating from the 1200s, Port-Sainte-Marie on the Garonne, which has a 13th-century church, and Buzet and Xaintrailles with their châteaux. From Nérac, you take the D656, turning on to the D136 for the 7 km ride to Espiens. Stay on the D136 for another 6 km, which brings you to Bruch. There you take the D213 for the 5 km ride to Saint-Laurent, turning left on to the D930 which takes you over the river to Port-Sainte-Marie. Then take the N113 to Aiguillon. For the return route, take the D8 for 6 km to Damazan and the D108 for a further 5 km to Buzet. Continue on the D108 for 8 km to Xaintrailles and a further 5 km to Lavardac before turning on to the D930 for the final 7 km to Nérac.

There are some pleasant rides of 30 km or so around Agen, which would give you a good taste of the surrounding countryside. A round trip of 25 km takes you first along the D305 to the Pont Garonne, 7 km away. There turn left over the bridge on to the C9 which runs alongside the Garonne to Sauveterre-Saint-Denis. Re-crossing the river here, turn left on to the C22 to Lafox and take the D215e to Saint-Amans. From there it is 3 km along the D269 to Bon-Econtre and another 5 km on the C206 to Agen.

Another journey of 24 km would take you to the château of Chadoits and through narrow country lanes to small out-of-the-way villages. From Agen take the N113 towards Bordeaux, turning right on to the D125 to Alary. Then take the C1 to see the 18th-century château, afterwards continuing along the road to Saint-Cirq and then turning right on to the D107 to Moulin-de-Mellet. Continue past the mill, turning left to descend into the valley. Turn left again by the stream and continue over the D107, turning east back to Agen on the road through Martel.

Bordeaux and the Garonne has much to offer, particularly to those with a sense of history—or to anyone who favours the Gascon's hearty approach to life and food. If you ever come across some of the locals at breakfast, you may well find them at a gargantuan feast, washed down by some of the region's splendid red wine. As you pass through the little villages and the walled medieval towns, you begin to wish that Talbot had not gone so recklessly into battle against Joan of Arc and that these foreign fields had remained forever England.

CHAPTER SIX

BEAUJOLAIS AND JURA

BEAUJOLAIS AND THE JURA lies north of Lyon, stretching across the sleepy valley of the Saône to the foothills of the mountains to the east. This is an almost forgotten corner of France, a country of lakes and flowers and fine cuisine. Wherever you cycle the glint of water will catch your eye, while the villages and towns vie with each other to show the most beautiful floral displays. The farmhouses, too, are often lavishly decked with flowers. Traditionally they are built of cob, with external staircases and distinctive overhanging eaves, as if they were wearing hats that were too large for them.

Like so many other parts of France, this is a region with a rich history. Its golden age came in the 14th and 15th centuries, when it was part of the great Duchy of Burgundy, whose dukes—Philip the Bold, John the Fearless, Philip the Good and Charles the Rash—were more powerful than the French king and among the most formidable figures of the age, sometimes siding with the English against the French in the dynastic struggles of the time. Their splendid court was a centre of creative and artistic life, particularly under Philip the Good (1419–67), when there was a great flowering of the arts.

Today, Beaujolais is more widely known for its wines and fine cuisine. The wines are world famous, although the vineyards have only been established for about 200 years, not nearly as long as in other parts of France. Much of the wine produced here—an unbelievable 130 million bottles—is an unpretentious light red, just right to accompany a lunchtime picnic. The finer Beaujolais Villages is a delicious wine, produced in 39 communes in the region. Finally there are the nine communes producing the best wines: Brouilly, which the locals describe as a wine for l'amour; Chénas, named after the great oaks (chênes) that once grew in the area; Chiroubles, produced from terraced vineyards; Côtes de Brouilly, from the yield of only a small area; Fleurie, one of the finest wines of the region; Juliénas; Morgon; Moulin-à-

Vent, generally thought to be the best Beaujolais; and St-Amour, a full-bodied but delicate wine. Beaujolais Nouveau, now the subject of an annual race to bring the first bottle back to England, is a wonderful quaffing wine in a good year, but painfully acid in a bad. There are also many delicious wines among the Jura vintages. The vineyards here are much smaller, producing wines of a wonderful golden colour, as if the locals have discovered how to bottle sunshine, and robust rosé wines such as rosé d'Arbois. There are also the unusual *vins jaunes*, as yellow as their name, which have a flavour similar to sherry. My favourite is a sparkling white wine called Étoile.

The cuisine of the region is equally renowned. The main elements are chicken, beef, trout, pike and perch, *escargots* and frogs' legs. *Coq-au-vin* and *boeuf bourguignon* are the two best-known Burgundian dishes, both owing much to the red wine in which the meat is cooked. Dishes tend to be simple, but they are usually based on excellent local produce and always cooked well. One of the great masters of gastronomy, the lawyer Anthelme Brillat-Savarin, was born at the aptly-named Belley, an ancient town in the Jura. His classic *Physiologie du goût*, concerned with the pleasures of the table, was published in 1824. The chefs of the region try to live up to his example and the city of Lyon and its environs to the south probably have the greatest concentration of first-class restaurants in France. Mouth-watering regional specialities include artichoke hearts served with *foie gras* and *la poularde demi-deuil*, in which the chicken has slices of truffles inserted under the skin and is then poached in a stock made from veal bones, leeks and carrots.

The simpler menus offered in rural hotels may well feature perfectly grilled fish, or the savoury *grattons*, browned particles of goose or pork fat spread on croutons or toast. The French delight in using every part of an animal and you may well find dishes such as grilled pigs' trotters and *le tallier de sapeur*, which is tripe coated with breadcrumbs, grilled and served with a *sauce tartare*. No one seems to know how the dish acquired its odd name, which a Frenchman once translated for me as 'a sapper's footboard'! Another such tasty dish is *salade Lyonnaise*, an hors-d'oeuvre which includes slices of pigs' trotters or calf's head and pieces of cold sausage, all seasoned with a dressing made of oil, vinegar and parsley. The plain of Bresse is famous for its free-range chickens, fed on maize. They can only be called Bresse chickens if they have been kept on grassland and they are a familiar sight, strutting in the fields. One of the greatest cooks from Lyon used to specify that the chickens used in her restaurant must come from the district of Louhans. *Soufflé aux foies de volailles de Bresse*, made with the local chicken livers, is a dish that, once tasted, is never forgotten. You will find plenty of cheeses made from goats' milk and the local *blue de Bresse*, a powerful blue-veined cheese. The desserts are among the most imaginative in France. And it is not only the cooking that is good; the presentation, too, is excellent. The chefs take great pride in the whole ambience that surrounds their restaurants.

Cycling in Beaujolais presents no problems. The plain of Bresse is a flat expanse of farmland. South of Châtillon towards Lyon is the area known as les Dombes, which is even flatter and a great deal wetter, full of lakes where fish and frogs are reared and wildlife abounds. Birds of many kinds flock here, so it is worth packing your binoculars. The mountains of Jura fringe the plains to the east and the hills of Beaujolais to the west. The scenery of these upland areas is very varied. In the Jura beautiful valleys with luxuriant pasture and woodlands become deep gorges cut by swift-flowing mountain streams. The hills of Beaujolais are not as high, but here too the scenery can be dramatic. Once into those hillier areas cycling can be uphill work, but the rewards—and your own sense of achievement—are enormous.

The climate is pleasant, particularly in early and late summer.

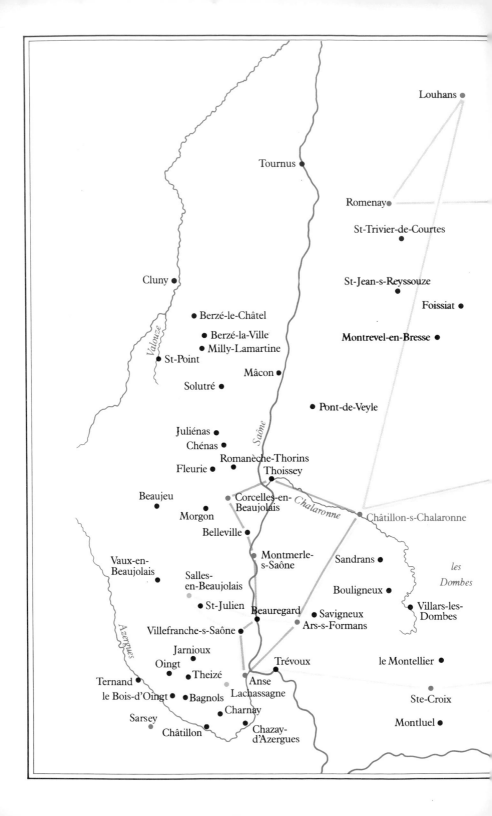

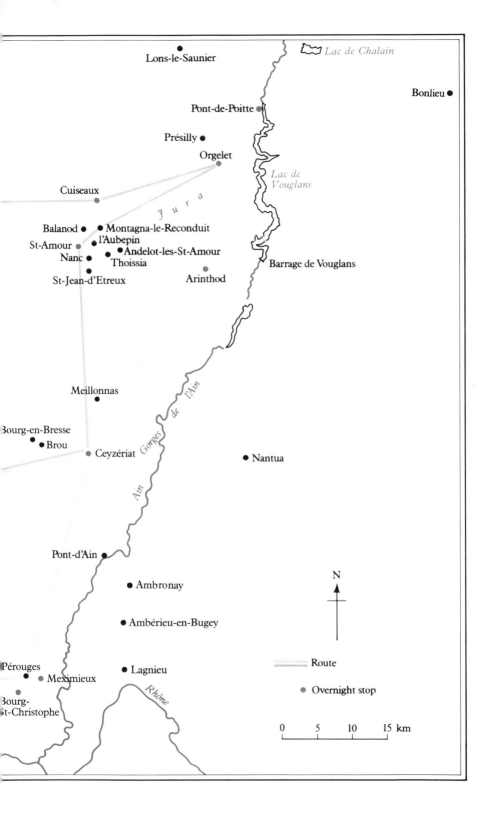

Lons-le-Saunier

Lac de Chalain

Bonlieu ●

Pont-de-Poitte ●

Présilly ●

Orgelet ●

Lac de Vouglans

Cuiseaux ●

J u r a

Balanod ● ● Montagna-le-Reconduit
●l'Aubepin
St-Amour ● ●Andelot-les-St-Amour
Nanc ● ●Thoissia

Barrage de Vouglans

St-Jean-d'Etreux ●
Arinthod ●

Meillonnas ●

Gorges de l'Ain

Bourg-en-Bresse ●
●Brou
Ceyzériat ●
● Nantua

Ain

Pont-d'Ain ●

N

● Ambronay

● Ambérieu-en-Bugey

Pérouges ●
●Meximieux
Bourg-St-Christophe ●

● Lagnieu

Rhône

═══ Route

● Overnight stop

0   5   10   15 km

From mid June to August it is hot and you may not wish to cycle long distances, although there are always lakes and streams where you can cool off. Spring and autumn are often delightful, with sharp mornings and evenings and sunny days when you feel you could keep going for ever, and when the sun is warming rather than crisping. The winters can be cold and there is skiing on the mountain slopes.

In a week you could tour the lovely gentle country to the south and west of Châtillon-sur-Chalaronne, the flower-filled town that forms a starting-point for exploring the region around Beaujolais, visiting Corcelles-en-Beaujolais, Montmerle-sur-Saône or Ars-sur-Formans and Anse. If you had more time you could go as far west as Sarcey on the edge of the Beaujolais hills and as far east as the gentle greenery of the countryside around Sainte-Croix. A fortnight's tour could take you from Châtillon-sur-Chalaronne to Ceyzériat, the outstanding medieval village of Pérouges, Sainte-Croix, Anse, Salles-en-Beaujolais and Ars-sur-Formans. You would also need a fortnight to explore the foothills of the Jura and the plain of Bresse to the north and east of Châtillon. With a first stop as before at Ceyzériat, you could go on to Saint-Amour, Orgelet or Pont-de-Poitte, Cuiseaux, Romenay and Louhans. A shorter tour to the edge of the Jura could take in Ceyzériat, then going south to Pérouges and Sainte-Croix and returning by way of Montmerle-sur-Saône to the west.

Châtillon-sur-Chalaronne, which lies between Mâcon, Bourg-en-Bresse and Lyon, is a thriving old market town, ablaze with flowers. They bloom from window-boxes, tubs and old tree stumps, hang from balconies, line streams and bridges and even fill boats floating on the river. The magnificent covered market in the centre of town is 80 metres long, with 89 tall wooden pillars and cross-beams supporting the sloping roof covered with the reddish-brown tiles of the region. It dates from the 1670s and replaced an earlier market burned down in a great fire that destroyed more than a hundred houses in the town. Nearby stands the plain and even older gothic church of St Andrew, built in the 14th century. The main road through Châtillon, the D936, runs straight across country, a clue to its Roman origins, but although Gallo-Roman remains have been discovered nearby, at the village of Fleurie to the north-west, Châtillon was settled much later. The brick-built Villars Gate, with its narrow arch, is almost all that now remains of the town walls, although many old houses survive.

The former hospital, a charming building, is now the cultural centre of the region. You can also visit the old pharmacy, which dates from the 1730s. Blue glazed and decorated Meillonnas earthenware pots which once held the drugs are ranged around the room on four tiers of wooden shelves. The pestles and mortars used to mix the medications, including an old, ornate bronze mortar, are also displayed.

One of the treasures of the town is a triptych dated 1527 showing incidents in the life of Jesus. The central panel depicts Christ being taken from the cross, while the two outside panels show him praying at Gethsemane while his disciples sleep, and his resurrection.

Across the river from the church you will find a statue of a priest with a child in his lap. This commemorates St Vincent de Paul, who was the village priest in the 1610s and founded the order of the Dames de la Charité to care for the poor. Nearby you can see the ramparts of the château that gave the place its name in the 10th century.

The town has five hotels. The one I favour is Au Chevalier Norbert in the centre of town, close to the market square (market day is Saturday). The hotel has recently been extended to include extra bedrooms in a lodge about 200 metres from the main building. The restaurant is excellent. Do leave room for one of the mouth-watering desserts, a memorable end to meals here.

There are many interesting excursions from Châtillon. To explore the south-east and the area of les Dombes, cycle 7 km along the D2 to Sandrans, where the unexpectedly grand church has an interesting interior that includes a carved pillar showing Adam and Eve with the serpent. Continue along the D2, with lakes on both sides of the road, to Bouligneux, which has a red-brick medieval château. A little further on is Villars-les-Dombes. The village church here dates from the 1300s, but the main attraction is its ornithological park around one of the lakes. This contains nearly 2000 birds of 350 different species in large aviaries or flying free. More exotic inhabitants include emus, eagles, penguins and pelicans and you can also see storks, the grey heron, the egret or white heron, many kinds of ducks, geese and visiting migratory birds.

Another gentle ride from Châtillon would be to visit Bourg-en-Bresse, 24 km away on the D936, where a market has been held every Wednesday since 1758. This delightful old town was settled in neolithic times and some prehistoric megaliths have been incorporated in later buildings. The Romans used them in their fortifications and the stones also formed part of the foundations of the prison, where they can still be seen in the basement today. After the Roman occupation, Bourg fell into decline until a castle was built on the ruins of the Roman fort in the 900s. This was replaced by a fortified village in the 1400s. Although its defences were later levelled, you can still see a few old wooden houses dating from the 15th century. Another reminder of the days of chivalry is Lices Square, the oldest part of town, which was used as a tilting yard by knights practising their martial skills for tournaments. The church of Notre-Dame, dating from the early 1500s, is well worth a visit, its five-tiered tower and spire rising dramatically at the end of a narrow old street. The window of St Crépin still has its medieval stained glass and there are fascinating carvings on the choir-stalls, providing a vivid documentary on the life of the time.

But a much greater ecclesiastical building lies at Brou, in what is now a suburb of Bourg only 1 km away. The monastery church here was started in 1506 at virtually the same time as Notre-Dame by Marguerite, daughter of the Emperor Maximilian of Austria, but it was finished in less than twenty years. By comparison Notre-Dame took more than a century to complete. The church at Brou was built with such astonishing speed to create a suitable setting for the tomb of Marguerite's husband, Philibert, Duke of Savoy, who died at the age of 24 after catching a chill when out hunting. It also fulfilled the vow made by Philibert's mother several years before that she would build a monastery if her husband survived a serious hunting accident. The church is a Flamboyant gothic masterpiece, a dazzlingly rich riot of carved wood and sculpted stone. The bible scenes portrayed on the choir-stalls are particularly intricate, with hundreds of detailed figures. This extraordinary building is an apt setting for the three magnificent white marble tombs it contains: of Marguerite, who died before the church was complete, after a cut turned septic; of Philibert, showing him both in his armour and as a worm-eaten corpse; and of his mother, Marguerite of Bourbon, the most elaborate of all. The church is now deconsecrated and the monastery next to it has been reduced to being used as a pigsty and as a lunatic asylum. Happily, some of its former dignity has been restored as it is now a museum displaying some fine examples of the enamelled jewellery that is a local speciality.

Philibert died at the Château de Pont-d'Ain, 20 km south. This was built in 1000 by the local barons and later became the home of the powerful dukes of Savoy. It is now used as a retreat for the priests of the region. Here too some old houses survive, clustered around the church.

The first overnight stop on a tour of the Beaujolais region is Corcelles-en-Beaujolais, a little village 21 km from Châtillon along the D7 and D9. The small Hôtel Gailleton here is recommended. On the way you will pass through Thoissey, where you can swim, or fish, in the Saône. You can also see horse races here on 14 July and 15 August. Corcelles is in the heart of the vineyards and there is a 15th-century château nearby where you can buy wine. Beaujeu itself, which gave its name to the area, is 17 km to the west, down winding country lanes. The wine villages of Chénas, Fleurie and Juliénas lie a few kilometres to the north and Morgon to the south and there are plenty of opportunities to visit cellars and taste the wine. For those with children there is a small zoo at Romanèche-Thorins 4 km north.

Romance can bloom among the vineyards here. A young doctor, sitting in the midday sun on a lush green hilltop, suddenly proposed marriage—although his intended was amazed when he leapt to his feet, tore off all his clothes and danced around her. 'C'est formidable', she said, 'I do, I do!' What she did not know was that he was sitting on an ants' nest.

From Corcelles go south-east to Belleville through Pizay, another small village with an 18th-century château. Like the other main towns of the region, from Mâcon to Lyon, Belleville stands on the banks of the Sâone, an attractive setting for an otherwise ordinary place, although it does have a 12th-century church.

Take the D17 across the Saône from Belleville and turn south for 4 km to Montmerle-sur-Saône. For those who would like an overnight stop, the Hôtel du Rivage here is in an idyllic setting overlooking the river. The more energetic could continue south for 12 km past Beauregard, where there is a manor house with two round towers set picturesquely on a wooded slope. Some 4 km east on the D904 is Ars-sur-Formans, a village that was put on the map in the early 1800s by Jean-Marie Vianney, a priest who was to become the patron saint of parish priests. A simple man, full of doubts, he nevertheless possessed a remarkable gift for converting people to Christianity and persuading them of the value of a religious life. His popularity grew to the point where he would spend 17 hours at a time hearing confessions. You can see the basilica built to house the relics of this saint, including an elaborate gilded bronze shrine in which his embalmed body lies open to view, and a chapel that contains his heart and a somewhat sickly statue of him praying on his knees. The village, which has no more than 700 inhabitants, is still regarded as a religious shrine and is visited by around 400,000 pilgrims a year. The Grand Hôtel de la Basilique is a good place to stay here. This old coaching inn is built around a peaceful, flower-filled courtyard, where you can sit and sip an early evening drink or laze the afternoon away with a book. The restaurant specializes in local food such as *escargots de Bourgogne*, in which the snails are served with parsley and garlic butter.

Just east of Ars, almost within walking distance, is an unusual church at Savigneux. The wide red-tiled porch over its main entrance is supported by four pillars carved with the faces of men and animals.

Ars is only 14 km away from the next stop at Anse to the south, a small town with a Roman fort and a 12th-century château. Close to the centre but away from the traffic you will find the Hôtel Saint-Romain, converted from an old farmhouse. On the way there I like to pause for refreshment in the market town of Villefranche-sur-Saône, which has a few old houses and interesting gargoyles on the church of Notre-Dame-des-Marais. Market day here is on Monday.

You can swim and enjoy water-sports at the lake at Trévoux, 5 km to the east of Anse along the D6. There are also the three broken towers of a ruined château here, the central one octagonal in shape.

An alternative to staying in Anse is the tiny Au Goutillon Beaujolais in the village of Lachassagne, a couple of kilometres to the south-west. The hotel stands in the middle of a vineyard owned by the proprietor and his son, from which they produce some delicious wine. On a clear day there are breathtaking views away to the east, sometimes as far as Mont Blanc.

The château at Lachassagne is one of many in the area and you could see several in a short round trip from the village. Another attraction of this part of Beaujolais is the honey-gold stone of the buildings, from which it is known as the country of the *pierres dorées*. A charming example of these 'golden stones' is the hillside village of Charnay, 7 km to the south down the D70. There is an impressive 12th-century church here with a painted stone statue of St Christopher dating from the 1200s as well as a ruined château. Then go south-east to the walled medieval village of Chazay-d'Azergues. The château here dates from the 1400s and has an unusual hexagonal tower. Cycle west from here through Châtillon, where the golden château set among green trees on a hillside glows in the sunshine. Look out for a gargoyle in the shape of a fierce dog which guards the turreted keep. To the west again, 5 km along the D485, is the château of Chessey-les-Mines, with its round keep dating from the 1100s, the same period as the earliest part of Châtillon. Return to Lachassagne through Bagnols. The 15th-century château here is not open, but the village has old houses and an interesting church.

An alternative outing from Anse or Lachassagne is the hilly ride 15 km west along the D39 and D19 to Theizé, where you can lunch well at the Restaurant l'Esperance. The medieval château of Rapetour is just outside the village. Continuing along the road brings you to Oingt, an ancient settlement perched high on a promontory in a sunny situation. Stone portraits of eight of the barons who ruled the place in the 1200s can be seen in the apse of the church. If you climb the 74 steps to the top of the castle tower, there is a splendid view over the vineyards of the surrounding countryside. For the return journey cycle 4 km south on the D120 to le Bois-d'Oingt, a village smothered in roses. A little further on, off the D13, is the Château de Flachère, built in the renaissance style. Unfortunately this striking building is not open to the public. Anse is now 17 km away and Châtillon another 34 km to the north.

You could also explore the Beaujolais area from Salles-en-Beaujolais, 20 km west of Châtillon. A tiny village in the hills, surrounded by vineyards, it has a 12th-century church that is regarded as the most interesting architecturally in the whole region. The Hostellerie Saint-Vincent here has its own swimming-pool, tennis courts and gardens.

To the north, 7 km away on the D35 and D49e, is Vaux-en-Beaujolais. This was the original Clochemerle, the famous fictional village created by Gabriel Chevallier in his witty satire on small-minded bureaucrats published in 1935. A second novel, *Clochemerle-les-Bains*, drew its inspiration from the pump-room where invalids went to drink the waters that once bubbled out below the village. Just south of Salles is the village of Saint-Julien, the birthplace of Claude Bernard, whose researches into the liver, the blood and the nervous system in the last century were of great importance. You can visit his house here.

From Salles you could go south-west to Sarcey on the edge of the Beaujolais hills. The Hôtel Chatard here is small and quiet, with a menu featuring lyonnaise specialities. For wine enthusiasts, the *caves coopératives* at Bully are only 5 km away, and there is a splendid viewpoint just outside the village. Alternatively, spend a quiet day fishing on the Azergues. A local *fête* takes place on 21 June each year. To reach Sarcey, take the D20, turning right on to the D504, a winding hilly road through wonderful scenery, and left on to the D485 at Chambost-Allières. Sarcey is off to the right after about 15 km.

Some 10 km north off the D485 is Ternand, which was the fortified home of the archbishops of Lyon. You can see the ruins of a keep and also a 15th-century church containing some old frescoes. Across country from here, some 12 km along a very windy road, is Jarnioux, with a renaissance château. You can head back south to Sarcey through Theizé and Bagnols.

Another wine-producing area within reach of Châtillon lies around Mâcon to the north. Known as the Mâconnais, it produces very good reds and whites, of which the Mâcon Villages is probably the most consistent. Stopping to sample the local wine at a vineyard in this area, one cyclist was mistaken for a buyer and given a guided tour. Even after he had explained the mistake, *le patron* insisted that he continue to taste the full range of wines. The road to Mâcon from Châtillon takes you through Pont-de-Veyle, an old town built between two arms of a river. Once walled, the original fortifications have almost entirely disappeared apart from a 14th-century gateway and the clock-tower. Mâcon itself is attractively situated on the west bank of the Saône, where the river is crossed by a restored 14th-century bridge. The old cathedral of Saint-Vincent was largely destroyed at the time of the Revolution and is now a ruin. Two of the several museums are particularly interesting. One contains prehistoric remains found at Solutré, a small village nestling under a high cliff about 8 km to the west on the D54. The bones of some 100,000 horses were discovered at the foot of the cliff here, thought to be the remains of animals that had been stampeded over the clifftop and then eaten by the early inhabitants of this area. Solutré is also the centre of the vineyards producing the white Pouilly-Fuissé wines.

The other museum, in a beautiful 18th-century house, is devoted to Mâcon's most distinguished writer, Alphonse de Lamartine, the 19th-century French poet and politician who was born here in 1790. An ardent royalist, he was very much at odds with his times. He is buried, together with his wife and daughter, at the village of Saint-Point, 25 km to the west. You can visit his manor house nearby, which he rebuilt in a romantic gothic style, and where his study is just as he left it. Two other places associated with him are just west of Mâcon. The Château de Monceau, where he lived in some style and had his own vines, is now an old people's home. A kilometre or so further on is the village of Milly-Lamartine, where he spent a happy childhood.

There are also some interesting religious sites in this valley. The monastic chapel at Berzé-la-Ville, a stone's throw from Milly-Lamartine, was a favourite retreat of the great St Hugh, abbot of Cluny. There is a marvellous 12th-century fresco here that was rediscovered under whitewash a hundred years ago. Nearby the medieval château of Berzé-le-Châtel rises above the surrounding greenery.

The abbey itself, or what is left of it, is a further 10 km to the north on the D980. Founded in 910, it was once the greatest monastery in Europe, a centre of intellectual and artistic life as well as a religious power-house. St Hugh, its most powerful abbot, began building a new church in the 1080s. The third on the site, it was the largest and most magnificent in Christendom, but only a century or so later Cluny's power began to fade. The abbey and its church were ransacked in the Wars of Religion and then partly demolished after the Revolution when the stones were used for other buildings and the abbey towers dynamited.

Even the very energetic would find this excursion through Mâcon to Cluny and back rather much in a day, as it covers a distance of about 100 km, so it is best to arrange to stay overnight, perhaps in Mâcon itself.

If you have a fortnight to spend in the area, Châtillon-sur-Chalaronne would make a good centre for a longer tour of the region. Go north-east from Châtillon to the pretty town of Ceyzériat, a distance of 30 km along the D936 to Bourg-en-

Bresse and the D979. The Hôtel Mont-July here is beautifully situated on the western edge of the foothills of the Jura, the spectacular mountain range which stretches east into Switzerland. The hotel is a short way out of the town along a back road leading up a hill called Mont-July. It is surrounded by a large garden and has a patio where you can relax on pleasant summer evenings.

There are many interesting places within reach of here, including the château at Pont d'Ain and Bourg (see p.142). Some 11 km south of Pont d'Ain is the ancient Benedictine abbey of Ambronay on the D36. It was founded in the 690s and its church dates from the 900s although additions and alterations were made over the next 600 years. Its shady cloisters are beautiful and there is also a gothic chapter-house. Most of the village's fortifications have now disappeared, with the exception of an old gateway, built in the 1200s. You can also take the train to Geneva for the day if you want a change of scenery and country. To the east, 40 km away on the D979, is Nantua, built at the end of a beautiful lake with mountains rising high around it. You can dine well on freshly-caught crayfish and there are enjoyable lakeside walks. But perhaps you should choose your transport to Nantua with care. A couple who took a little local train here were surprised when it stopped 10 km short of their destination. Stranded on a rapidly emptying station in the pouring rain, only the kindness of the station master, who gave them a lift into town in his car, saved the day.

Along the D52, 8 km to the north of Ceyzériat, is the village of Meillonnas, famous for its faïence, tin-glazed earthenware pottery which was first made here. The man responsible was Gaspard de Marron, who set up a pottery in the outbuildings of his château in the 1750s. The original pottery went out of business more than a hundred years ago, but other potters here continue to create faïence in the traditional way, usually decorating the pots and plates with painted flowers: carnations, forget-me-nots, marguerites and roses. You can visit the workshops and wander along the unspoilt old village streets.

From Ceyzériat go south to the astonishing hilltop town of Pérouges, a ride of 46 km down the D42 and D984. You could make a detour east on the way to see the Château des Allymes at Ambérieu-en-Bugey, a square red-brick building which houses archaeological and historical exhibitions. South of Ambérieu is the Château de Sainte-Julie at Lagnieu, which is particularly noted for its beautiful ceilings. Pérouges is straight across country from here.

Pérouges is a fantasy place, a medieval fortress with cobbled streets, a huddle of red-tiled half-timbered houses and a massively threatening church. Apart from the fact that the buildings are far from new, it seems to have hardly changed since it was built. Its stolid ramparts remain, as do two narrow gateways. Not surprisingly, its medieval splendours have been captured on many historical films.

I tend to stay not in Pérouges itself, but in either the village of Bourg-Saint-Christophe or the busy market town of Meximieux, both a couple of kilometres away. The Hôtel Chez Ginette at Bourg-Saint-Christophe is a little rural *auberge*. Locals throng into the bar from early morning and it can be a little disconcerting drinking coffee at breakfast while all around you are swigging brandy. You can swim in the lake and the river there and the village festival is held on the third and fourth weekend in July. Meximieux is a smart, bustling little town. In the centre of it is the Hôtel Lutz, which has an excellent restaurant.

It is well worth visiting the Grottes de la Balme from here, some 20 km south-east along the D65, D123 and D20. These are some of the most spectacular caves in France, with cavernous cathedral-like spaces and fantastic stalagmites and stalactites.

One of the caves is filled with the still, clear waters of an underground lake.

The next stage is a short ride across country to Sainte-Croix, only some 11 km away. You could make a longer ride along the D4 and D61 to see the fine château at Montellier, but this can only be admired from the outside. Sainte-Croix is a tiny village which is ideally situated for visiting the southern part of les Dombes and even Lyon if you feel like a day out of the saddle. There is virtually nothing at the village except the excellent Hôtel Chez Nous, where the good food will certainly revive you.

From Montluel, 5 km to the south along the D61, you can take a train to Lyon, France's second largest city, particularly noted for its superb and expensive restaurants, its many museums and its centuries-old silk industry. Standing at the confluence of the Saône and the Rhône, it has been a city of great strategic importance throughout the history of the region.

From Sainte-Croix you strike west for 34 km to Anse (see p.145), along the D4 and D6 through Trévoux. After Anse, you head north to Salles-en-Beaujolais (see p.147) along the scenic D70 and the D43 from Villefranche-sur-Saône, a journey of 20 km. For the final stretch you cross the Saône once again to Ars-sur-Formans (see p.144), 8 km east of Villefranche, from where Châtillon is 20 km north-east along the D936.

An alternative fortnight's tour could take you north and east into the foothills of the Jura. Starting from Châtillon the first stage would be to Ceyzériat as before. From there you could head north to Saint-Amour, a journey of 33 km. This little market town on the edge of the Jura, once torn apart by through traffic, has been saved from ruin by a by-pass. The small Hôtel d'Alliance close by the market-place is recommended. It is an old building with a most unusual interior. The town is also ancient, the houses clustered around its tall clock-tower. Two crumbling ivy-covered gateways still stand and you can walk around the remains of the town walls. There are delightful views from here across the plain of Bresse to the west, which from this vantage point seems as vast and blue as the sea. The church, which dates from the 1400s, is built on the site of a Roman temple. A small white building topped by a bell and a cross next to a ruined round tower was once the hospice and pharmacy of a former Capucin monastery.

There is a delightful 20 km round trip from here. Ride north on the N83 to Balanod, 3 km away, turning right on the D51 for another 3 km to Montagna-le-Reconduit, set in rocky countryside pierced by deep gorges and with many little waterfalls. Turn right again on the D3e to Thoissia, which is another 5 km, and then take the D3 on the right for 3 km to l'Aubepin, where there are the ruins of an ancient castle and the hermitage and chapel of Saint-Garadoux. Continue along this road for 4 km to return to Saint-Amour. For a slightly longer excursion turn left on the D3 along a winding hilly road to Andelot-les-Saint-Amour, where there is a splendid example of a typical medieval fortress. Another ancient château survives just south of Saint-Amour, at Nanc. If you take the D185 from there for 5 km you come to the village of Saint-Jean-d'Etreux, a delightful spot from which there are further spectacular views of the surrounding countryside.

The more ancient farmhouses on the plains to the west of the Jura are notable for their Saracen, or *Sarrasin*, chimneys, which are shaped like spires or tiny minarets. Such chimneys can be seen on thirty farms in the area. They are found nowhere else in France and no one can explain their significance, although it is possible they were intended as status symbols.

Rather than just looking at the plain of Bresse spread out below you, you could visit the Saracen farmhouses at Saint-Trivier-de-Courtes and Montrevel-en-Bresse. Saint-Trivier, which is 22 km to the west of Saint-Amour along the D56 and

D2, is an attractive village with old wooden houses and a 15th-century church. Just before it, you take the road on the left to the Ferme-de-la-Forêt, a two-storeyed half-timbered old farmhouse. A balcony shelters under the overhanging roof with its pointed Saracen chimney. The house contains an exhibition of rural life in times past. Just beyond Saint-Trivier, take the D80 for 7 km down a quiet road through woods to Saint-Jean-sur-Reyssouze, a charming village decked with flowers and with an 11th-century church that is being restored. Montrevel-en-Bresse is 10 km down the D975 from here. The farmhouse, which you can visit, is 2 km to the west of the village. It has a rather baroque mitre-shaped chimney. Another typical farm, which cannot be visited, is at Foissiat, 17 km to the west of Saint-Amour, along the D1 and D1e.

The next stop from Saint-Amour is Orgelet, 30 km to the north-east by winding roads through the hills. The little village of Cuisia between the two has a well-preserved 15th-century château. The countryside here is magnificent, with dramatic views. Orgelet itself has a fortified church built in the 1400s. There is a market on the second Wednesday of every month and a village festival on 15 August. The pleasant Hôtel de la Valouse on the edge of town has a set menu that changes every day and a most delicious array of puddings.

South of Orgelet, 17 km down the D109, is the stone-built village of Arinthod, which lies in the beautiful valley of the river Valouse, providing some of the most memorable scenery you are likely to see. The main street here is arcaded like so many others in this part of France. If you want to stay overnight, the tiny Hôtel de la Tour in the main square is recommended. The village church dates from the 1500s and has a Gallo-Roman stone depicting a Gallic god fixed on an exterior wall. There is a good excursion east of here along the D3 to the spectacular gorge cut by the Ain. Another 4 km further along the D60 and you arrive at a huge dam, the Barrage de Vouglans. You can swim in the broad, long lake that has been created behind it.

The rich history of this area is evident in the museum at Lons-le-Saunier, 20 km to the north of Orgelet. It contains a neolithic dugout canoe, some 10 metres long, found at the Lac de Chalain to the east of Lons (15 km away along the D471 and D39, by roads through thick woodland). Lons is a charming town and, with more than 23,000 inhabitants, large by local standards. Claude Rouget de l'Isle, the French army officer who composed the rousing *Marseillaise*, was born here and there is a statue of him in full song. In the old part of town the Rue du Commerce is lined with arched arcades, providing welcome shade in the height of summer. The hospital, which dates from the 1700s, has elaborate wrought-iron gates. Inside, you can see a display of the pottery that was once used to hold drugs. Two old churches are also worth visiting: the simple Saint-Desiré, which dates in part from the 1000s and contains a fine 15th-century carving of Jesus being laid in the tomb, and the church of the Cordeliers, which was built two centuries later. Lons is also known for the hot springs which, it is claimed, will cure many illnesses, including digestive ones! On the way back from Lons make a detour right on the D52 to see the château at Présilly, where there is a *son-et-lumière* during the summer months.

The lake created on the Ain fills the valley for several kilometres behind the dam. From the high and modern Pont-de-la-Pyle, 5 km to the east of Orgelet, there are spectacular views down its length. A village on the Ain, Pont-de-Poitte, is an alternative stopping-place north of Orgelet along the D470 and D49. Indeed, while the front of the Hôtel de l'Ain faces on to a little square, its back almost tumbles into the river. Beside the hotel is a shop specializing in jewellery and ornaments made from bone and horn where you might find some small souvenirs for family and friends back home.

For a really dramatic sight cycle east from Orgelet or Pont-de-Poitte along the D67 and N78. Just north of Bonlieu the river Hérisson cascades down a narrow gorge in a series of waterfalls—the Cascades du Hérisson. You can clamber over huge boulders to stand very close to the water, foaming white as it falls from high above your head. Woodland crowds in all around.

For the next stop you travel back west to Cuiseaux, 6 km north of Saint-Amour, another old town surrounded by the remains of its walls and peaceful now that a by-pass has been opened to take the cars and lorries from its narrow streets. The small Hôtel du Commerce here has been run by the same family for three generations, and has an excellent restaurant. Another good hotel, the Hôtel du Nord is, as its name suggests, on the northern side of town. The locals celebrate their festival on 7 July. Like Saint-Amour, Cuiseaux would also be a good base from which to explore Bresse and its ancient farmhouses, which you could see on the way to the walled town of Romenay, 5 km north of Saint-Trivier-de-Courtes. Romenay's Hôtel du Lion d'Or has a restaurant serving succulent local specialities. Other attractions are houses dating from the 12th century and a small museum.

You could go directly from Romenay to Louhans, 19 km north-east, but it is worth making a detour, or a day trip, to Tournus, an ancient town delightfully situated on the river Saône with medieval and renaissance houses and cobbled streets. It is totally dominated by the lovely church of Saint-Philibert, one of the earliest and best-preserved romanesque churches in France. The present church was begun on the site of an earlier building at the end of the 10th century and took a hundred years and more to complete. Not surprisingly, it was fortified. From the outside it suggests power; inside, though, it has an uncluttered simplicity of light and line, enhanced by its pink stone pillars. Perhaps the monks' fear of attack explains one of the carvings, which shows a priest giving a blessing with one hand while holding a large hammer in the other.

Another interesting place is the Hôtel-Dieu, which dates from the 1600s, an attractive building with a fine collection of earthenware in its pharmacy. Two museums are worth visiting: the Musée Perrin de Puycousin, housed in a 17th-century mansion, which is a folk museum, and the Musée Greuze, which has drawings and paintings by Jean Baptiste Greuze who was born in the town in 1725. This rather sentimental painter enjoyed international popularity for a time, but died in poverty at the age of 80. No doubt he would have appreciated having his works hung in a former convent.

Louhans is also an attractive town, with a main street fronted by elegant arcades. Louhans' Hôtel-Dieu and L'Apothicaire, reminders of the care of the poor and sick in the Middle Ages, almost rival the magnificent examples at Beaune, some 60 km or so north, in the centre of the vineyards of Burgundy. The roofs of these buildings are patterned with many-coloured glazed tiles arranged in geometric shapes, a style that was once common in the region. Market day is Monday, when the corn-fed chickens bred hereabouts, their flesh bathed in milk, are on prominent display. Many will be served up as *poulet de Bresse à la crème*. The town festival is held in the last week in August. The Hôtel du Cheval Rouge is recommended.

At Louhans it is worth abandoning your bike for a day and taking the train north to Dijon, famous for its mustard but notable for some fine old buildings and excellent restaurants as well. The dynamic dukes of Burgundy, the dynasty begun by Philip the Bold in 1364, ruled their immense domain from this ancient city; the magnificent tombs of two of them can be seen in the superb art museum housed in their former palace, which faces a semicircle of elegant old buildings in the Place Royale. Not far away is the gothic church of Notre-Dame, with a clock-tower on which mechanical figures strike the hours and quarter-hours. The early 14th-century cathedral of Saint-Bénigne is also largely gothic, although the crypt dates back to the 11th century and the church still has its original romanesque doorway. The streets of the old town are full of pleasing domestic architecture, from half-timbered buildings to renaissance masterpieces, often with patterned roofs of coloured tiles. For the thirsty, an appropriate drink here is *kir*, three parts chilled white wine to one of *crème de cassis*, a liqueur made locally from blackcurrants. It is named after a former mayor of the city who insisted that it was the only aperitif provided at civic functions.

From Louhans you could make your way south back to Châtillon some 69 km away. Stay overnight at Saint-Amour or Bourg if you want to break the journey.

CHAPTER SEVEN

THE RHÔNE VALLEY

THE VALLEY OF THE RHÔNE is a land of rivers. The Rhône itself is broad and sparkling, an important traffic artery busy with barges and cruisers and with towns and villages dotted along its banks. Two major tributaries—the Drôme and the Isère—flow into it from the east, fed by icy mountain waters. In their upper courses these rivers have carved deep and spectacular gorges before emerging from the uplands to meander across the meadows and through the gentle green orchards which border the Rhône. Numerous lesser streams and rivulets provide welcoming coolness on hot summer days. Warm and well-watered, the land yields up an abundance of vegetables and fruit, with trees heavy with cherries, apricots and peaches in summer. You will also see orchards of walnuts, grown to make the famous nougat at Montélimar.

This is one of the most beautiful and restful parts of France. The back roads winding across the countryside are very peaceful, yet full of wonderful surprises and unexpected sights and pleasures. 'I had forgotten about hedgerows and butterflies', one visitor to the area told me on his return. Another remembers cycling along with nine butterflies perched on the front of his

bike. Wherever you go, the prospect is never monotonous.
Every distant horizon is bounded by striking mountain scenery.
To the east there is the wild region of the Vercors, a stronghold
of the Resistance during the Second World War. This is dramatic
walking and climbing country, which merges with the Alps on
the borders of Italy. West of the Rhône is the imposing plateau of
the Ardèche, another wild landscape. There is spectacular
cycling through these areas for the energetic, or easy rides along
the many gentle river valleys on the plain below. In the
undisturbed lanes you are more likely to be delayed by sheep and
goats than you are by cars or tourists. There are extensive
forested areas too, particularly to the south where this region
shades into Provence and the landscape becomes more
Mediterranean in character. Here there are a number of *villages
perchés*, built in places that were easy to defend, often on dramatic
hilltops. Some of these villages are recommended as places to
stay and they do involve a short sharp climb at the end of the
day—but it is never more than a kilometre or so.

Above all this is wine country, as it has been for centuries
since Greeks first brought the vine here in the 6th century BC.
Vineyards now cover a very large area and the number of wines
produced is considerable. Most are red, spicy and full-bodied,
even the everyday Côtes du Rhône. The smallest vineyard,
Château Grillet, which lies between the towns of Condrieu and
Roussillon, produces only a few dozen bottles a year and can
claim to be among the rarest wines in the country. Probably the
best is the deep red Côte Rotie from a nearby vineyard. Some
excellent whites, as well as reds, come from l'Hermitage opposite
our base town of Tournon.

The food in this region of France tends to be simple and well-
cooked, mixing the Burgundian dishes that gained Lyon its
reputation as a gourmet's paradise with the spices and herbs of
Provence and the traditions of the Auvergne and Languedoc. If

you are lucky, you may be offered roast woodcock or guinea fowl, braised wild boar, jugged hare, hare pie and chicken with crayfish, although regional tastes also encompass roast thrush and ortolan. Local chestnuts are used to flavour dishes and are fed to the pigs to enhance the taste of pork and ham. Many too are grown to be turned into mouth-watering *marrons glacés*.

With so many rivers in the region, fish are abundant. The popular local dish known as *pouchouse* is a sort of freshwater version of the *bouillabaisse* of Marseille, a fish stew based on carp, perch and pike cooked in white wine and garlic. Menus frequently feature eels from the Rhône, often served up cooked in red wine as *matelote d'anguilles*.

People have lived around the Rhône since prehistoric times, and have left their paintings and engravings of the animals they hunted in several caves in the region. Standing stones, too, remain as evidence of their occupation. The Romans later conquered the local tribes, although only a few signs of their empire have survived. This area of France suffered terribly in the Wars of Religion between Catholic and Protestant in the 16th century, as the many ruined châteaux and fortified villages bear witness. In the last hundred years there has again been depopulation, following the decline of the two principal industries, mining and silk manufacture.

A word of warning. Temperatures in the Rhône valley can be very high. On average the sun shines for 300 days every year and in summer it beams down powerfully from a blue and often cloudless sky. If you can, plan your cycling in May, June or September.

I like to explore the region from Tournon, a lovely old town with a ruined château, narrow streets and Europe's oldest suspension bridge. One nice feature is its railway, which follows the valley of the Doux into the Ardèche.

In a fortnight of gentle touring in the Rhône valley from

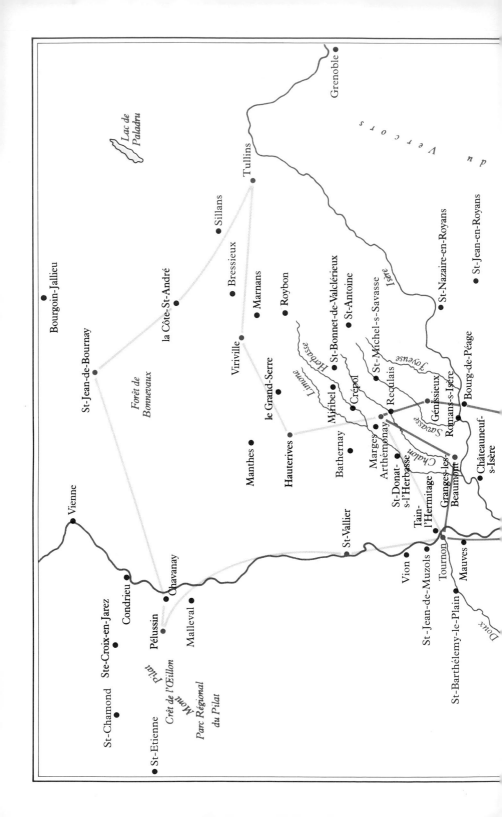

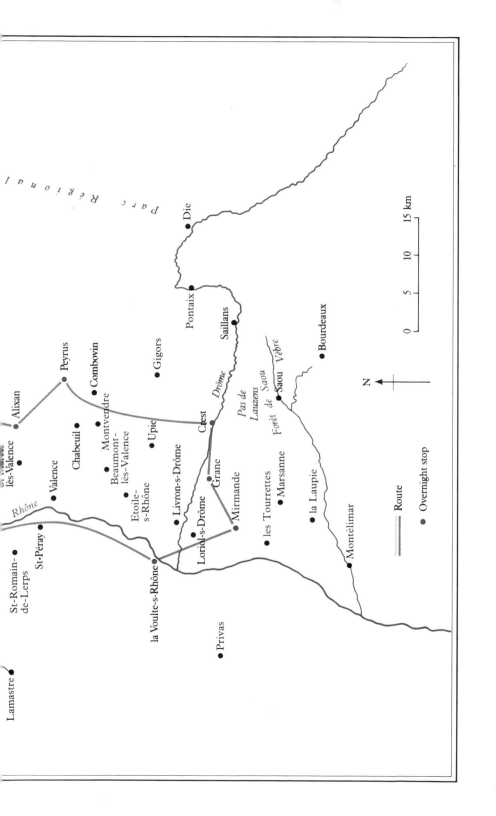

Tournon, you could visit some of the most famous vineyards and the undulating farmland around Granges-les-Beaumont, Arthémonay, Génissieux, Alixan, Peyrus, Crest, Grane, Mirmande and la Voulte. Some of the suggested stopovers are only a short ride from each other and you would have plenty of time to take in the sights, or just to laze the days away. If you have only a week to spare, a shortened tour could take you to Granges-les-Beaumont, Arthémonay, Génissieux, Alixan and Peyrus.

In a fortnight you could also explore the valley of the Isère running north-east from Tournon. The suggested tour to Arthémonay, Hauterives, Viriville, Tullins, Saint-Jean, Pélussin and Saint-Vallier takes you into beautiful hill country and you would need to tackle the occasional climb.

With luck, you will also have an adventure or two, like the cyclist who, having trouble with the back wheel of his bike, stopped off to buy some wine and discovered that the merchant's son was the local hill-climb champion with a fully equipped bike workshop. He not only repaired the bike but invited the traveller to lunch. Later that same day, the wheel began to give trouble again. This time the cyclist went into a café to discover where there was a bike shop. The owner made several telephone calls until he located someone who could help, invited the traveller home to dinner and took him for a wine-tasting in his cellars before driving him to his hotel.

Tournon is the western half of twin towns that straddle the Rhône. On the eastern bank is Tain-l'Hermitage, which is always known as Tain, its famous vineyards climbing steeply from the river to a height of some 300 metres. If you come to Tournon from the Tain side of the river, all you have to do is cross the bridge and you are there. You can also wheel your bike across a little footbridge that brings you out opposite the two most important hotels in town, the Hôtels du Château and Paris, which are both run by the Gras family.

The town is administratively, culturally and geographically part of the Ardèche and the locals refer to themselves as *Ardèchois*. An ancient place, where even the high school dates back several hundred years, Tournon is virtually untouched by developers and many of the streets are closed to traffic. The château overlooking the town, built in the 1500s, seems to grow out of the high rock on which it stands. It now houses a museum mostly devoted to local history and the history of transport on the Rhône. From this vantage point you can look across the bend of the river and the town below to the hill opposite covered by the vineyards of l'Hermitage, with a tiny chapel standing in the midst of them. To the east you can see the grandeur of the Alps. The town's collegiate church of Saint-Julien contains some 400-year-old frescoes that have recently been restored. The old school is also worth visiting, with its charming quadrangle and a collection of tapestries from Flanders and Aubusson. Stéphane Mallarmé, the Symbolist poet, taught English there in the 1860s. You can swim in a good pool in Tournon or at the riverside beach along the Doux just out of town. Market day is on Saturday.

Cycling through the surrounding countryside involves a certain amount of hill-climbing, but the rewards are spectacular views of the Rhône glinting between tree-covered hillsides. A varied 42 km round trip takes you along the river and also up into the hills. Go south for 3 km along the N86 to the village of Mauves, famous for growing the small onions used to make *oignons à la greque*, cooked in olive oil and served cold as an hors-d'oeuvre. This is also the area which produces the somewhat unpredictable wine of St-Joseph. The old village church at Mauves contains a 16th-century statue of the Virgin. The Rhône begins to widen here as it approaches the dam at Glun, which is 3 km further south. Continue to Saint-Péray, another 12 km further, passing the medieval château at Châteaubourg on the way. At Saint-Péray it is well worth making a little detour of a kilometre or so to see the ruins of the Château de Crussol, perched on a rocky crag. Climb to the top to look over the river valley stretching beneath you. Return to Saint-Péray and take the D287 into the hills to Saint-Romain-de-Lerps. If you have any breath left after the climb, you will gasp at the panoramic view across the Rhône to the snow-capped Alps. The road brings you back to the N86 just beyond Mauves from where it is a short ride back to Tournon.

There are several interesting villages to the north of Tournon. Some 3 km along the N86 is Saint-Jean-de-Muzols, an old port that dates back to Greek and Roman times although the river has now retreated from it. Travelling a further 4 km north of the village brings you to Vion, another place that has been left high and dry by the Rhône. The fertile alluvial land is now covered with cherry orchards. The local vineyards produce a pleasant white wine which you can drink in the village. It is also worth visiting the church. Built from 1040, it contains some fine carvings in wood and stone and a crypt that predates the rest of the building.

To the west, 10 km away on the D532 and D238, is Saint-Barthélemy-le-Plain, high in the mountainous region above Tournon on the route to Lamastre. There are spectacular views across the pine-clad hills from the road winding up the valley. Unless you are very energetic, though, you can enjoy the scenery from the *Lou Mastrou*, the little steam train that makes the 33 km journey from Tournon to Lamastre through the Doux valley and which will do all the puffing for you. The line was built in the 1880s and closed in the 1960s, but some enthusiasts clubbed together and reopened it, using locomotives that are more than 80 years old. Lamastre is a two-hour ride through spectacular wild countryside, ending in a Mediterranean landscape cut by deep gorges. The old train chugs over bridges and viaducts, past vines and orchards, as it climbs steadily up the valley, stopping at tiny stations along the way. Sights to look out for are the Château de Chazotte on the right and the so-called 'trembling rock' just before the viaduct at Arelbosc. At Lamastre itself a barrel organ plays on the station. During the summer months, the train usually leaves Tournon at 10.00 am and sets out on the return trip at 4.00 pm. Lamastre has a ruined château and a church that dates from the 1100s.

Anyone who has read Emmanuel Le Roy Ladurie's *Carnival of Romans* will want to see the place itself. Ladurie tells the extraordinary story of how the citizens of Romans-sur-Isère set up a kind of workers' republic in the 17th century, and how it was suppressed after fierce resistance. The town, which is 15 km east of Tournon along the D532, owes its origins to a monastery founded by Saint-Barnard in the 800s. It is now a bustling market town, famous for shoe-making, sprawled along both sides of the Isère. The church of Saint-Barnard, which has a romanesque porch and a gothic choir and chapels, dates from the 1100s, although parts were added and changed until the 16th century. The clock-tower was part of the building's early fortifications. There are also two unusual and interesting museums in Romans. The first, housed in a former convent, is devoted to the Resistance fighters of the Second World War. The other is a shoe museum containing a collection of footwear from all over the world that spans a period of a thousand years. Folk-singers and dancers gather in the town for a festival at Whitsun and there is a contemporary music week in July. Bourg-de-Péage across the river has some pleasant public gardens.

We tend to stay not in Romans itself but in one of the villages nearby, such as Granges-les-Beaumont, 7 km away. This tiny hamlet consisting of a few houses, vineyards and orchards set in rolling green countryside also contains the Hôtel Restaurant Lanaz, where the cuisine is highly regarded. The guest-rooms are in a pavilion in the garden behind the old hotel.

The back roads here are delightful and very quiet. You can take them to travel 5 km south to Châteauneuf-sur-Isère, a small village on the south bank of the river which has some troglodyte houses cut into the hillside. To reach it, turn right on the D196 after crossing the Isère and left at les Beaumes.

Arthémonay, 16 km north of Romans along the D538, is a gentle ride from Granges-les-Beaumont. There you will find the Auberge le Pont du Chalon. This is well known locally for its *boules* team, who can often be seen playing on the ground opposite the hotel. Regional specialities are served in the restaurant, including a local variation on ravioli made with goats' cheese that is served as a starter, *pognes*, a sweetbread smelling of orange, and guinea fowl and quail.

Some 9 km west of Arthémonay is Saint-Donat-sur-l'Herbasse, noted for its Bach festival from the end of July to the beginning of August. Its collegiate church, which has a fine organ, dates from the 1100s, although it was added to in the 15th century; the chapel of Saint-Michel contains some ancient wooden statues of the apostles. You can go swimming, boating or engage in water-sports at the nearby lake of Champos. Colourful striped umbrellas along the lake shore provide welcome shade.

The countryside around is dotted with fascinating old villages, often with a slightly battered charm. You can visit the prettiest in a round trip of about 28 km, almost entirely on little-used back roads. From Arthémonay go north-west on the D583 to Marges, continue north for a further 1.5 km and then turn right on to the D67 for 3 km to Crépol. Continue along the road for another 4.5 km to Miribel, just off to the left on the D513. Return to the D67, turning immediately right for a 3 km ride to Saint-Bonnet-de-Valclérieux. From here the D155 runs 12 km to Reculais, a couple of kilometres south of Arthémonay.

Part of the charm of this region lies in the frequent little valleys of the five rivers that cross it—the Joyeuse, Savasse, Chalon, Herbasse and Limone. East of Arthémonay is Saint-Michel-sur-Savasse, 12 km away, where you can enjoy good swimming and fishing. Bathernay, a village in a pretty region of hills and valleys, is about the same distance north-west. One curiosity of the village is the Auberge des Grottes, built, as its name suggests, in a cave.

Staying in another small village, Génissieux, brings you just north of Romans-sur-Isère. The pleasant small Hôtel la Chaumière in Génissieux, run by a mother and daughter, is recommended. To the east, 9 km away, is Saint-Nazaire-en-Royans, a small port prettily situated by a broad canal. The town is a cluster of old houses around a high-arched aqueduct with a church dating from the 1200s. It is surrounded by wooded hills and you can see high mountains in the distance. Just outside town is la Grotte du Thais on the D531, once inhabited by prehistoric peoples. South of Saint-Nazaire, 9 km away on the D76, is the attractive Saint-Jean-en-Royans, which is a tourist centre for exploring the dramatic heights of the Vercors.

Alixan, a village of around 100 houses with a handsome old church and some ancient fortifications, lies 8 km south of Romans. It is a delightful place where we stay in the Hôtel de France. Cherries, peaches, melons and other summer fruits are grown in this area and if you are here at the right time of year there is blossom everywhere. You will also see walnut plantations and are likely to come across farmers selling home-made goats' cheese.

From Alixan you can visit Valence, the largest town in the area, some 10 km south-west down the D171. Both Rabelais and Napoleon studied here, one at the university, now no more, the other at military college. Valence has Roman origins, though you would hardly know it these days, for it has grown considerably in recent times. Handsome boulevards stretch down to the river, where you can look across to the ruins of the Château de Crussol, stark on its clifftop. You can wander in a large and beautiful park and along the pedestrianized streets at the centre of town. Despite its modern suburbs, Valence still has beautiful old houses at its heart, especially along the Grand-Rue. Look out for the curious, ornate House of Heads in this street, decorated with weathered carvings. The cathedral of Saint-Apollinaire, built in the 1090s, has suffered over the centuries and was much rebuilt in the 1600s. Not far away is the Pendentif, a renaissance chapel. The former bishop's palace now houses a museum which has exhibits on local history as well as a collection of paintings from the 16th century onwards. You can also see the distinctive red-chalk drawings of romantic ruins by Hubert Robert, the 18th-century artist who was one of the first curators of the Louvre. Summer fairs are held in the town during July and August. The small Hôtel-Restaurant Pic, which is south of the town on the N7, has a national reputation for the excellence of its cuisine, but it is, as you would expect, expensive. Of the many other restaurants, I suggest you try La Licorne.

A trip to Valence could form part of a 35 km tour from Alixan. Head south to Chabeuil on the D538, a busy little market town noted as the home of the local speciality known as *caillette*, quail cooked with herbs and dry white wine and stuffed with pork meat and liver. Market day is on Tuesday. Strike out across country along the D236 for 9 km from here to Beaumont-lès-Valence, a small village where you can swim and play tennis and visit an interesting church. From Beaumont, it is 8 km to Valence along the D538a and then a further 10 km back to Alixan. Those interested in vintage cars could extend the tour to Saint-Marcel-lès-Valance on the N532, where more than a hundred old cars are on show at a museum.

Wherever you stay near Romans, it is worth making the trip

to Peyrus, a little village in the foothills of the Vercors. You can approach it from Alixan either via Chabeuil on the D538, turning left on to the D68, a total distance of 16 km; or by cutting across country, taking the D101 from Alixan to Bésayes and then going right on to the D102 through Charpey. This is a somewhat shorter ride. Peyrus stands on one of the few good roads into the Vercors and is a popular holiday centre with the French, who come here in July and August. The Hôtel du Commerce et du Parc is recommended and there is a local pool where you can swim. If you can manage a climb of 14 km up to the Col des Limouches on the D68, 1086 metres above sea-level, the view of Peyrus and the Rhône valley is quite magnificent.

Crest is 28 km south of Peyrus along the D538, at the beginning of the spectacular valley of the river Drôme. You could make a slight detour on the way to Montvendre, a short distance left on the D176, where the Auberge le Vieux Moulin, which specializes in fish, serves excellent food. 'In Britain we would have paid at least four times as much,' one visitor told me; he described his meal—the 90-franc menu—as probably the best he had ever had. Some 6 km further on you could turn right on to the D538ᴬ and then immediately left to Upie, where the riverside Jardin aux Oiseaux has more than 1000 birds of 200 different species, ranging from owls and vultures to ostriches, ducks and pelicans. A tougher but very beautiful alternative route from Peyrus to Crest would be to cycle by way of Combovin and Gigors along the D732, a distance of 40 km.

Thrusting into the sky on a hill above Crest is a massive stone tower, 52 metres high, which is all that remains of a fortress which Louis XIII ordered to be destroyed in the 1630s. This hugely powerful medieval keep, the tallest in France and one of the finest in Europe, is dramatically illuminated at night. You can climb up the tower for a panoramic view of the surrounding area and of the old town beneath it. Festivals are held on 29 June and

20 September and there is a jazz festival every July. Market days are Tuesday, Wednesday and Saturday. The Grand Hôtel in Crest lives up to its name with its magnificent marble staircase.

To the south lies the great Forest of Saou. For a ride full of rural delights, take the D538 for 13 km to Saou itself, where a ruined château still dominates the old village, and then turn left on to the D136 for 3 km, turning left again on to the D70 to ride through the forest over the Pas de Lauzens, between the valleys of the Drôme and the Vèbre. The view as you come down from the top of the pass is quite stunning. (There are also spectacular views over the valley of the Roubion if you do this ride in the other direction.) Continue for 10 km to Aouste-sur-Sye, from where Crest is another 3 km on the D93. If you continue on along the D538 for 24 km without turning left at Saou, you come to the interesting village of Bourdeaux, which was a centre for the Resistance during the Second World War. This is a pleasant place with a number of old houses, some dating from the 1400s, and its setting is beautiful. Like so many other villages, it is dominated by its château, now a ruin.

A ride 37 km east of Crest following the river Drôme brings you to Die. You could follow the D93 all the way, but it is much more enjoyable cycling along the minor roads on the south side of the valley. The little river villages of Saillans and Pontaix have houses perched precariously over the water. Die itself is a delightful old town, founded by the Romans and famous for its Clairette de Die, a sweet sparkling wine. Some ancient fortifications and a triumphal arch still survive, and Gallo-Roman remains can be seen in the museum. The cathedral was built in the 1100s and rebuilt in the 1600s after being much damaged during the Wars of Religion. The mountains of the Vercors rise up spectacularly all around Die and it is well worth staying here and taking a day out of the saddle to follow some of the many footpaths.

The exceptionally attractive village of Grane lies on the other side of the valley from Crest. It is a mere 9 km on the D104, but it is well worth stopping here to sample the cuisine at the Hôtel Giffon, which is renowned. The village is built on a steep hill and the hotel is in the main street right at the top. You can swim in the river Drôme. During June jazz concerts are held in the village and there is a festival on 15 August. Market day is Thursday.

There are many excellent excursions from here. To the north-west, 19 km on the D125, D93 and D555, is the fortified hilltop village of Étoile-sur-Rhône, which dates from the 1400s and has a romanesque church. There are good views from the village over the Rhône and to the Vercors. You could return by way of Livron, another old town to the south. This too is set in a delightful part of the river valley. A Protestant stronghold, it suffered during the Wars of Religion, as its ruined church testifies. Its château is curiously sited on the town ramparts. You can swim in the Lac des Petits Robins here.

The sweet-toothed will want to make the 30 km journey to Montélimar, world-famous for its nougat. Although the town was much damaged during the Second World War, there is far more to it than its jaw-breaking sweet. The old part of Montélimar has some medieval buildings and a house dating from the 1500s said to have belonged to Henry II's powerful mistress Diane de Poitiers. The remains of the ruined castle of Mont-Adhémar brood over the town. Across the Rhône, 5 km away on the D11, is another great ruin, the castle at Rochemaure, spectacularly sited on a hilltop overlooking the river. There are also the remains of a medieval village here and there are stunning views of the river valley from the top of the hill.

To the south of Grane, 16 km on the D113 and D105, is the ancient fortified village of Marsanne, where you can see the old priory of Saint-Felix. The road takes you along the edge of a splendid forest. Another 4.5 km to the south, on the D129, is la

Laupie, an old village which has been wonderfully restored.

The next stop is Mirmande, 9 km south-west of Grane, an ancient *village perché* perched up above the Rhône valley. The village is set precipitously on a steep hillside, with flights of stone stairways connecting the old houses and workshops. The church crowning the top of the hill dates from the 1100s. The view from here looks down over what have been called the most beautiful roofs in France. A colony of artists settled in the village from the 1930s, attracted by the influential critic and Cubist painter André Lhote. The Hôtel la Capitelle is in a lovely golden stone building dating back several hundred years. To the south, 7 km away, is another medieval village, les Tourrettes, which has the ruins of a château and the medieval chapel of Saint-Didier.

Hemmed in on one side by the Rhône and on the other by the hills of the Ardèche, la Voulte-sur-Rhône is 20 km from Mirmande, reached by travelling west on the D57 and N104 and then north on the N86. Its château dates from the 1400s and was greatly damaged by German troops in the 1940s. The river broadens out here and you can go sailing or canoeing on it. There is also an excellent local pool. The Hôtel le Musée is recommended.

To the south-west, 20 km along the N86 and N104, is the pleasant small town of Privas, capital of the Ardèche and an important centre for producing *marrons glacés*. You can take a hard and longer ride back across the hills along winding roads, well worth it for the spectacular views. From la Voulte Tournon is only 32 km north along the river.

The second route takes you further north of Tournon, stopping first at Arthémonay, some 20 km away (see p.170). This is probably most easily reached by way of Saint-Donat along the D115, D67, D121 and D583. From there you go north on the D538 for 14 km to Hauterives. A ruined château and the comfortable Hôtel Restaurant le Relais are among the attractions of this town buried in woodland. But the great curiosity is the bizarre Palais Ideal built by the local postman, Ferdinand Cheval, who died in 1924. His palace is an extraordinary creation that people travel hundreds of miles to see. It is one of those rare buildings that can make you laugh for the sheer pleasure and madness it evokes. It is not surprising that it was much admired by Surrealist artists. M. Cheval collected pebbles and oddly shaped stones as he went on his rounds and spent his evenings for more than thirty years cementing them together in his garden to create a dreamlike building of strange crenellated towers and slender turrets. When he completed it, he spent ten years building himself a tomb in a similar style.

The building has a childlike quality of an imagination untrammelled by reality, of an inspired doodle in concrete and stone. Little staircases lead nowhere in particular; irregular columns bulge in unexpected places; tiny figures stand on top of tall minarets; parts are festooned with stalactite-like excretions; and others are covered by what looks like petrified vegetation. There is nothing quite like it anywhere else.

Hauterives has a village festival on the last Sunday in August and a market on Tuesdays. You can swim in the local pool and play tennis on nearby courts. Some 6.5 km east—go along the D51 and then bear left on the D66—is le Grand-Serre, a village with a 10th-century church and an 11th-century market, surrounded by the Forest of Chambaran. You could go from here along the D137 to Manthes, where the old church has a stained-glass window dating from the 1300s. Hauterives is 10 km south.

The old town of Saint-Antoine lies to the south-east, a journey of 30 km by way of the D20 to Roybon, turning right for a ride through the forest on the D20^B. The town is dominated by the gothic abbey church of Saint-Antoine. Building began in the 1200s and continued for two hundred years to create what was once a powerful abbey, where popes and kings came on pilgrimage. Among its treasures is a 16th-century ivory carving of Christ.

The next stage of the tour is to Viriville, 30 km to the north-east of Hauterives, where there is another ruined château. Travel along the D51 for 20 km, turning left on to the D156d. In the centre of the village is the little Hôtel Bonnoit, an excellent establishment where the vegetables served in the restaurant come fresh from the hotel garden. Market day is on Tuesday and there is a village festival in mid August. Sometimes you can see the work of local artists who paint on silk.

To the south-east, a ride of 4 km on the D156c, Marnans is a tiny, otherwise unremarkable village with a fine romanesque church. To the north of Viriville, 14 km along the D130 and D71, is the hilltop town of la Côte-Saint-André, where you can visit the house where Hector Berlioz was born in 1803. It is now a museum containing memorabilia of the composer, including the flute, clarinet and guitar which he learned to play in his youth. The old château was rebuilt in the 1600s, but there is an interesting old 16th-century market building and a church dating from the 1100s with a colourful tower. On the way back continue past the junction of the D130 and D71 to see the ruins of the château of Bressieux on the left, stark on a rocky outcrop above the village.

At the edge of the foothills of the Vercors, 29 km to the east, is Tullins, a small town full of wooden buildings and decorated with masses of geraniums. To reach it, go north on the D156, turning right on to the D519. Some 2 km past Sillans, turn right on to the D73e. We like to stay at the Auberge de Malatras on the N92, in the direction of Vinay, about 1.5 km out of town. It is a bit of a climb to get in and out of Tullins, but the scenery is memorable and worth all the effort and there are delightful walks along the Isère. North of town, 20 km away on the D50, is the beautiful Lac de Paladru known, for obvious reasons, as the Blue

Lake. This is a mecca for windsurfers and other devotees of water-sports during the summer.

The very fit will enjoy the cycle path through the hills for 25 km to Grenoble, but it is also possible, and less exhausting, to visit this big city by bus or train. If you do go there, then you must ride the cable-car that takes you to the Fort de la Bastille on a clifftop more than 475 metres above the city. From this vantage point you can see Grenoble spread out before you in its river valley, surrounded by forests and high mountains. Much of the city is new and it is still growing, but there is also a fascinating old town, with a 10th-century cathedral, as well as one museum devoted to the writer Stendhal, who was born in the city in 1783, and another with a superb collection of modern art.

Saint-Jean-de-Bournay to the north-west of Tullins is an unspoilt little town with an ancient keep set amid green and fertile countryside. It is a ride of 44 km from Tullins, the last stretch through the lovely woods of the Forêt de Bonnevaux. Stay in the Grand Hôtel du Nord, which faces on to the town square. Market day in Saint-Jean is on Monday, and you can swim and play tennis locally.

From Saint-Jean you could visit Vienne, 23 km to the west along the D502, which still displays many signs of its Roman and medieval importance. A large Roman theatre has been excavated and plays are staged there. Other Roman remains include a temple of Augustus and Livia, built in the first century BC and restored in the 19th century, and a Roman arch, and there are also traces of the town walls. The cathedral of Saint-Maurice is a fine mix of romanesque and gothic styles, full of intricate ornament and some splendid stained glass, although it has been damaged during various religious uprisings. The church of Saint-André-le-bas dates from the 800s and there is a museum of ecclesiastical sculpture just off its cloister. Saint-Pierre is even

older, with foundations dating from the 300s. Much altered over
the centuries, it now houses a museum of sculpture and Roman
mosaics. The town also contains some medieval houses, their
upper storeys jettied out over the streets.

To the north-east of Saint-Jean, 16 km along the D522,
Bourgoin-Jallieu is a less interesting town, although it was there
that Jean Jacques Rousseau, that most itinerant of philosophers,
wrote part of his *Confessions*. The Musée Victor-Charreton
contains paintings by artists with local connections.

Reaching Pélussin, the next stop, involves a fairly stiff climb,
since it is up in the Ardèche. The Hôtel de l'Ancienne Gare is
very welcoming at the end of the ride. A distance of 50 km,
Pélussin is best reached not straight across country but by
travelling first to Vienne along the D502 and then going south
to Chavanay. Here you turn right on to the D7 which climbs up
into the hills. The effort is once again rewarded by the
extraordinary beauty of the surroundings, with tiny villages full
of flowers buried among the wooded slopes. This area has been
designated as the Pilat National Park, after Mont Pilat which
rises above Pélussin to the west. It is a haven for wildlife and you
may see foxes, boar and deer here. From Pélussin with its old
château and chapel you can also look east over the valley of the
Rhône and the vineyards of St-Joseph.

As an example of the kindness often offered by the hoteliers,
some visitors staying at the Hôtel de l'Ancienne Gare were asked
by the owner one hot and sticky evening if they would like to go
for a ride in his van to the high Crêt de l'Oeillon for a spectacular
and cooling view. Together with his wife and daughter and two
waitresses, they sat on the dining-room chairs in the back of the
van and rattled off, only to find that the road was blocked. So
they stopped off at a nearby hotel, where *le patron* insisted on
buying everyone a glass of cider.

The major town of this region is Saint-Etienne, at the foot of

Mont Pilat, which you can reach by going north on the winding
D62, and then down the D88, a ride of 35 km. Some 8 km
outside Saint-Etienne you pass Saint-Chamond, with its
medieval castle and the ruins of a Roman aqueduct. The ride
there is considerably more enjoyable than arriving at the town,
since, as the slag heaps show, it is a large mining and
manufacturing city with only a good theatre and plenty of
sunshine to recommend it to visitors. The museums concentrate
on mining and industry.

To the south of Pélussin, 10 km on the D79, Malleval is an
old, fortified village with houses dating back to the 1400s. It has
an interesting ancient sheep enclosure as well as yet another
ruined castle. The ride to it is dramatic, for it is built on the edge
of a deep gorge. Just past the village a little river gushes over the
rocks in a delightful waterfall.

There is another magnificent ride on the D62 to the north of
Pélussin. Turning right on to the D7 and left on the D30 brings
you to Sainte-Croix-en-Jarez, where the charterhouse was built
in the 1200s and abandoned at the time of the French
Revolution.

Down in the Rhône valley, Condrieu, 13 km from Pélussin on
the N86, is a pleasant old river port with a zoo just outside town.
A good white wine is produced from the vineyards on the
hillside above.

Saint-Vallier, the final stopping-point before the return to
Tournon, is 34 km south beside the Rhône. It is best to cycle
along the small roads on the east bank where you can avoid the
traffic. The Hôtel des Voyageurs where we like to stay is in the
centre of the town, tucked away in a courtyard. Saint-Vallier is
well supplied with small shops, with several selling *charcuterie*
and enticing *pâtisserie*, and you can swim in the local pool. Henry
II's celebrated mistress Diane de Poitiers spent part of her
childhood at the château in the early 16th century, although she

was not allowed to remain a child for long as she was married at the age of 13. Unfortunately, the château is not open.

From Saint-Vallier it is a 16 km ride south to Tournon. Again, it is best to cycle along the small roads on the east side of the river, a route that takes you through the vineyards and orchards that are such a memorable feature of this magnificent countryside.

CHAPTER EIGHT

PROVENCE

THE VARIETY OF PROVENCE is stunning. From its rocky coastline to the mountains, valleys and plateaux in the north, it is a sublime country. Villages of golden stone perch on rocky outcrops. There are green meadows, peach and cherry orchards, and wild, untamed landscapes, from the watery vistas of the Camargue to the jagged limestone of the Alpilles. Part of the special character of the area derives from the quality of the light, and the intensity of colour. The sky is brilliantly blue, the stone blindingly white or richly yellow-brown, tiles a deep and satisfying red.

And everywhere there are memories of a rich and varied past, from the palace of the popes at Avignon to the immense sweep of the ancient Pont du Gard and the echoing vastness of the Roman arenas at Nîmes and Arles. The Greeks came to Provence in 600 BC, settling at Marseille which has remained a major port ever since. But it was the Romans who stamped a permanent imprint on the region, not only naming it but creating a road system that is still visible and leaving a rich legacy of architectural remains. Then, when the papacy was based at Avignon in the Middle Ages, Provence was once again a focus of cultural and artistic life.

The climate is Mediterranean. The summers are hot, with temperatures around 25°C during the day and deliciously warm evenings; winters are mild. Provence is particularly appealing in May, June and September, when the weather is often superb without being scorching. In winter and early spring, though, the cold, north wind known as the *mistral* can be bitter and there may be torrential rainstorms.

For me, the most fascinating area of this region of France is perhaps the Camargue, whose mysterious beauty has captured the popular and artistic imagination only recently. Once it was thought to be too primitive, a trackless marsh inhabited only by wild, white horses and black bulls and by the Camargue cowboys, *les gardiens*. Now its wild charm has been recognized, and the national park at its heart protects its unique character. On its western edge, the walled city of Aigues-Mortes, built as a planned settlement in the Middle Ages, still has its original grid street pattern and still evokes the atmosphere of the 13th century. Inland, vineyards reach up to rocky crags where ruined castles and stony villages perch watchfully over the watery plain.

Another part of Provence I love is the plateau of the Vaucluse, an area of luxuriant valleys and limestone hills riddled with caves, where gorse, lavender and thyme grow on the lower slopes. Then there are the historic towns of the Rhône valley, Arles, Avignon and Orange, set in an area that includes some notable vineyards. Almonds, olives, melons and, above all, grapes grow here. Grapes to eat and to be turned into the strong, warm and sometimes fiery wines for which Provence is famous.

The most southerly vineyards of the Côtes du Rhône are at Avignon. Vines were first grown here by the Greeks more than 2500 years ago. The internationally famous Châteauneuf-du-Pape comes from a village just north of Avignon where Pope John XXII built a new castle (*château neuf*) in the 1300s. Although grapes had been grown here before this date, the vineyards began to acquire their reputation from this time under the patronage of the popes.

Gigondas is another powerful, dark red wine of the area, but two of my favourites are Tavel (especially the rosé) and Lirac. These both come from vineyards across the Rhône from Châteauneuf-du-Pape. The wines are said to get their special quality from rocks in the vineyards acting rather like night-storage heaters—absorbing the sun's rays during the day and giving off warmth during the hours of darkness.

The distinctive flavours of Provençal cuisine come from the many herbs of the region and the fruits of the olive. Provençal specialities include *terrine de la mère Anna*, made from chicken, rabbit and pork, *artichauts à la Barigoule* and *civet de porcelet aux herbes de Provence* (which one local restaurant translates as 'piglet stew', a description that hardly does justice to the casserole of tender meat flavoured with aromatic herbs). Another hearty favourite is *daube de boeuf à la provençale*, a casserole of beef cooked in red wine flavoured with crushed garlic and thyme, with a sauce made from anchovies and capers added towards the end of its cooking.

Fish also frequently features on the menu, fresh from the sea or the many rivers. You can eat sea bass grilled over stalks of fennel, or the mouth-watering *bourride*, in which the fish is poached in stock and served with *aïoli*, Provence's famous garlic mayonnaise. Then there is *bouillabaisse*, the Marseille fishermen's soup made from whatever they happened to catch, or, perhaps, from what they could not sell, but containing at least half-a-dozen varieties of fish, all flavoured with olive oil, garlic, onions, tomatoes and herbs.

One of the pleasures of the early summer months is *soupe au pistou*. This can be made from all sorts of vegetables, but always includes white and broad beans, flavoured with fresh basil, garlic, puréed tomatoes and parmesan cheese. And there is the ubiquitous *salade niçoise*, made with salmon, anchovies and the local black olives—much the same ingredients as are found in the sandwiches served in the local cafés. For the sweet-toothed, there are *calissons*, the little diamond-shaped, iced and almond-flavoured biscuits made in Aix-en-Provence.

It is not surprising, perhaps, that the combination of climate, landscape, light and food has attracted so many artists to Provence. Van Gogh, Cézanne, Fragonard, Picasso, Braque, Léger, Chagall and Gauguin have all painted here. Writers include the poet Frédéric Mistral, who created epic verse in the local dialect and won the Nobel Prize for Literature in 1904, the playwright and film director Marcel Pagnol, whose best work was set in Marseille, and Jean Giono, whose novels deal with peasant life in Provence.

As ever with cycling, there is also the unexpected. One couple were sipping their wine in a quiet café in Lagnes when the peace was shattered by a huge piece of agricultural machinery moving past. The café owner became very excited and urged them to follow it and return to pay him later. It was, he said, the world's first automated cherry-picking machine. They followed it, together with most of the villagers, to a nearby orchard. One part of the machine consisted of a huge stretch of canvas attached to a conveyor belt; the other had two arms which gripped a tree and shook it until the fruit fell free on to the canvas. The machine shook the tree to which it was attached once and then broke down. It was back to the drawing-board—

and back to the café for another reflective glass of wine.

Although inland Provence has some notable summits and spectacular scenery, this is not a region which will overtax the casual cyclist. There is easy cycling in the Camargue and through the vineyards and orchards along the Rhône, while even in the hillier areas routes tend to follow river valleys rather than striking across ridges. The steepest stretches are likely to be climbing up to the many villages perched on defensive sites, known as *villages perchés*. These relics of a turbulent past are characteristic features of Provençal scenery, dramatically crowning hilltops and crags. So you may have to walk the last kilometre or so to some of the overnight stops, or if you want to enjoy a good meal in the middle of the day.

The energetic could take in both Provence and the Camargue in a week's fairly hectic cycling, an experience that might tax the unfit at the height of summer. A tour from Avignon, returning to the city a week later, could take in stops in Saint-Rémy-de-Provence, Maussane-les-Alpilles, Arles, l'Albaron, Saint-Gilles and Pont du Guard, visiting Nîmes en route. A less taxing week through Provence to the north-east of Avignon would be to explore Pernes-les-Fontaines, Caromb and Venasque and the interesting places around them.

If you have a fortnight, a good tour including the Camargue but also taking in the wilder country to the west of the Rhône would take you from Avignon to Barbentane, Arles, l'Albaron, Aigues-Mortes, Sommières, Uzès and Pont du Gard. Or if you prefer to go further east in Provence, a fortnight could take you from Avignon to Pernes-les-Fontaines, Venasque, Joucas, Lauris, la Barben, Cornillon-Confoux, Maussane-les-Alpilles, Saint-Rémy-de-Provence and Barbentane.

Avignon itself makes an excellent centre for a holiday, since it is well placed to reach a variety of scenery and places of interest. Avignon is known as the City of the Popes—so-called because a

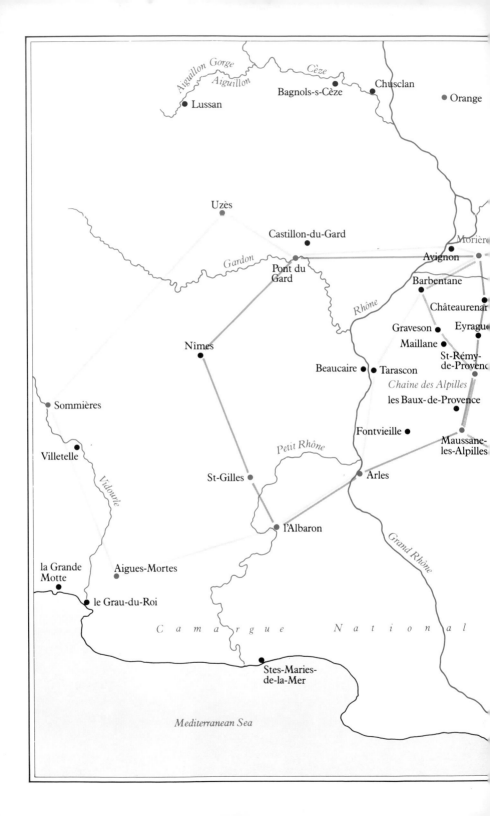

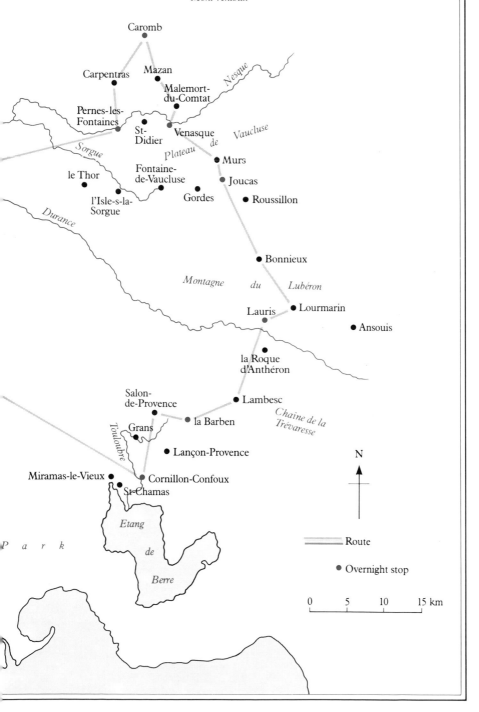

Mont Ventoux

Caromb

Carpentras   Mazan
             Malemort-
             du-Comtat
Pernes-les-
Fontaines   St-
            Didier   Venasque   de   Vaucluse
                                          Plateau
Sorgue   Plateau   Murs
le Thor   Fontaine-
           de-Vaucluse   Joucas
           l'Isle-s-la-   Gordes   Roussillon
           Sorgue

Durance

Nesque

Bonnieux

Montagne   du   Lubéron

                  Lauris   Lourmarin

                                    Ansouis

                  la Roque
                  d'Anthéron

Salon-
de-Provence   Lambesc
Grans   la Barben   Chaine de la
                             Trévaresse
            Lançon-Provence   N

Miramas-le-Vieux   Cornillon-Confoux
            St-Chamas

            Etang

P a r k   de

            Berre

            ════════ Route

            ● Overnight stop

            0   5   10   15 km

French pope moved the papacy here in the 1300s when Italy was wracked by war. It remained the centre of papal power under six more French popes. As a result, Avignon became a city of great importance, the centre of the Christian religion. Merchants and bankers as well as artists, musicians and nobility were attracted here and this was undoubtedly Avignon's golden age. The popes eventually moved back to Rome, but they left a legacy of fine buildings which greatly enriched the city.

Avignon is still at heart a basically medieval town. It is always vibrant with life and almost bursts its seams in July during its arts festival. Its famous bridge, the Pont Saint-Bénézet (who has not sung *Sur le Pont d'Avignon*?), now reaches only a little way across the river, having been a ruin for 300 years. There is a tiny ancient chapel dedicated to St Nicolas on one of its piers.

The vast papal palace stands on a rock overlooking the river. It is a sprawling building fortified with walls 3 metres thick which seems to have been designed to no particular plan. The 12th-century cathedral stands nearby, overshadowed by the Rocher des Doms, the rocky outcrop that dominates the town. It is worth climbing to the garden on the top for a marvellous view over the city. Of the town's many other attractions, one of the most memorable is the Musée Calvet, housed in a beautiful 18th-century building. This is an exceptionally good provincial museum, displaying French paintings. There are plenty of hotels to choose from in Avignon itself, but I prefer to stay in the recently-built Hôtel le Paradou in Morières-les-Avignon, a village about 7 km east of the city.

From Avignon there are interesting excursions to Orange and Bagnols-sur-Cèze in the Rhône valley to the north. Orange, a Roman city later sacked by barbarians so that only the theatre and a magnificent arch remain, is 25 km from Avignon. Its theatre is in remarkable condition, considering its age, forming a graceful amphitheatre that is still used to stage plays and concerts. The triumphal triple arch, built more than 1900 years ago, celebrates Roman power and is richly decorated with scenes of their exploits. Some fourteen centuries later Orange was linked to another foreign power, in this case the Dutch noble house of Orange-Nassau, from whom the town takes its name. It remained independent of France for a hundred years, but was reclaimed by Louis XIV from William of Orange, the Dutchman who was to rule England with his wife Mary after James II abandoned the throne.

Bagnols-sur-Cèze is due west of Orange, but you have to go a little way downstream to cross the river and, except for the energetic, it is probably best visited on a separate trip from Avignon, 28 km away. An ancient town with houses that date back to the 1600s, Bagnols has a good museum of modern art containing work by French Impressionist painters, including Monet. Some 6 km to the south-east is Chusclan, a village that leads to a panoramic view of the Rhône and the lands around it.

From Avignon south to Saint-Rémy is a journey of some 20 km that takes you first through Châteaurenard, a market town. Its two medieval towers, all that remain of a fortress destroyed in the French Revolution, provide splendid views of the surrounding area. If you are travelling from Morières, your route could take you past the Chartreuse de Bonpas, where the church was built by the Knights Templar, the militant religious order, from the 1200s onwards—although the chapter-house dates from the 1600s. Alternatively, you could make a detour east from Châteaurenard. Cycle on through the village of Eyragues and you arrive at Saint-Rémy-de-Provence, which has a few Roman buildings that escaped the destruction of the barbarian hordes who invaded the province in the 200s. There is a mausoleum that honours Caius and Lucius Caesar, the young grandsons and heirs of the Emperor Augustus, and the ruins of a commemorative arch.

Saint-Rémy is also closely connected with Van Gogh. The former monastery of Saint-Paul-de-Mausole just outside the town is where the great painter went in 1889 after cutting off his ear, to be treated in the asylum there. Despite several breakdowns, he continued to paint until his suicide a year later. His cell can still be visited.

The excavations at Glanum, just beyond Saint-Paul-de-Mausole on the D5, have revealed occupation by the Gauls and the Greeks as well as the later Romans and several temple sites have been uncovered. Many finds are displayed in Sade House, a museum in the town. More everyday items are on show in the Pierre de Brun Alpilles Museum, housed in a 16th-century mansion, which displays collections of regional costume and furniture. You can also see the house where the astrologer and seer Nostradamus was born. A good place to stay is Hostellerie le Chalet Fleuri on the edge of Saint-Rémy, on the road to Maillane. This little hotel is surrounded by a colourful garden where you can sit and enjoy dinner—the chef cooks Provençal specialities—in the shade of spreading plane trees.

The next stage takes you a short journey along the D5 through the spectacular Chaîne des Alpilles, an area of jagged limestone peaks and rocky ravines between Avignon and Arles. The bare rock gleams white in the bright light, appearing snow-covered in the height of summer. The D5 runs through the mountains, past slopes wooded with pine, through orchards of cherries and apricots to Maussane-les-Alpilles, a small town on the edge of this savage country. In a square in the centre of the town is the Hôtel l'Oustaloun, which has had every interior surface, from door-panels to the backs of chairs, delightfully decorated by its owner, who is an artist.

The nearby village of les Baux-de-Provence, the archetypal Provençal hilltop settlement, is well worth a special trip from Maussane, or a detour on the way there. You reach it either by

turning right on to the D27 for a 2.5 km ride before arriving at
Maussane, or by cycling back from the town, which adds another
2.5 km to the journey. Les Baux is built on a narrow rocky
outcrop that falls away steeply on all sides, a perfect site for an
impregnable medieval fortress that has now dwindled to a ruin,
destroyed 300 years ago by the French king. Two hundred years
before, it had been the custom to throw the hapless victims of the
barons who lived there down the ravine. The village's more
modern claim to fame is that it has given its name to bauxite, the
clay from which aluminium is made, which was discovered
nearby. Les Baux has to be explored on foot and includes an
extensive area of ruins, known as the dead village. The White
Penitents' Chapel, which dates from the 1600s, contains modern
frescoes by the Provençal artist Yves Brayer. There are also
magnificent views over the surrounding countryside.

The next stage is through a gentler landscape, along the D17
for 18 km to Arles, passing Fontvieille and the abbey of
Montmajour on the way. At Fontvieille, a small quarry town,
turn left on to the D33 to see the windmill where the novelist
Alphonse Daudet spent the winter of 1863–4 for reasons of
health and wrote some of his best stories, which were later
published under the title *Lettres de mon moulin*. You can either
return to the D17 or continue 2 km further along the D33 to
some ruined Roman aqueducts which once supplied Arles and a
nearby mill with water. Turning right on to the D82 will bring
you swiftly back to the D17 and the fortified abbey of
Montmajour, which dates back in parts to the 900s. The blue-
grey buildings stand on a small hill which was originally an
island in a sea of swamp, but is now fringed by rice-fields. If you
have the energy to climb the hundred or so steps to the top of the
abbey tower, you will be rewarded by a splendid view.

A further 7 km along the D17 and you arrive at Arles, which
also makes a good centre for exploring the Camargue and the

western part of Provence. Arles is now very much a tourist centre—there are over 100 hotels and more than 20 camping sites in a town of 50,000 inhabitants—but it is an amazing place. Architecturally, it is extraordinarily rich, a legacy of its former importance as the capital of Roman Provence and of a period of considerable prosperity in the Middle Ages. Here you can see not only a major Roman amphitheatre, but also a fine renaissance town hall.

The Roman amphitheatre at Arles was turned into a fortress in the 1100s and the towers erected then still stand. Once an arena where gladiators fought each other and wild animals to the death, it is still the scene of fierce combat, as bullfights are now staged here, featuring the black bulls bred in the Camargue. The remains of the Roman theatre form a stage for plays and opera during the summer months.

The other reminder of Roman occupation is Les Alyscamps, a place where the Romans buried their dead and which continued to be used as a burial ground until the 1100s. It is lined with elaborate tombs, though the best have been destroyed or removed and the church is a ruin.

Despite its pagan memories, Christian roots run deep here. In 597, Saint Augustine was consecrated as the first Bishop of Canterbury in the splendid church of Saint-Trophime, after his success in converting the English to Christianity. Although much altered in the 11th, 12th and 15th centuries, the church has a magnificent doorway and a cloister richly decorated with carvings of saints.

Today, Arles is also known as a centre of the arts, celebrated in the vigorous festival held every July. The fascinating Museon Arlaten, which owes much to the generous support of the local poet Mistral, is given over to a collection of Provençal arts and crafts. There are museums devoted to Christian and pagan art and the Musée Reattu, in what was once the priory of the

Knights of St John, contains a good collection of modern art, including paintings by the Provençal artist Brayer, Fernand Léger and Henri Rousseau and drawings by Picasso. Van Gogh spent two years living and painting in Arles, producing some of his best-known work, although the two houses in which he lived were destroyed during the Second World War. It was in this city that he severed his right ear and from here he moved to the mental asylum housed in the former monastery of Saint-Paul-de-Mausole.

There are numerous places to stay in Arles, catering for all pockets, but the Hôtel d'Arlatan can be recommended.

The next stage of the tour takes you into the Camargue, the great area of marsh and plain stretching away to the west, savage and lonely. An easy ride of 15 km along the D570 brings you to l'Albaron, off the beaten track in the middle of the Camargue National Park which extends from Arles to the Mediterranean at Saintes-Maries-de-la-Mer. There are few buildings, apart from a ruined fortress, and virtually no shops, but it is an ideal spot for admiring the many wild flowers and watching the bird life, which includes herons, waders, ducks and all manner of waterfowl, as well as the ubiquitous flamingoes. I have even seen a hoopoe. You may find binoculars and a pocket-book on birds a help. Although l'Albaron is so small, it includes the Hôtel le Flamant Rose, where you can stay. If you feel like abandoning the bike for a day or two you can hire a horse and trek through the marshes, or take the bus which passes the hotel to Saintes-Maries-de-la-Mer, 23 km away along the D570. The port has been immortalized in Van Gogh's painting of sailing boats on the shore here, but is much better known for its twice-yearly *fêtes*.

In late May and around October 22, gypsies and the Camargue horsemen gather at Saintes-Maries-de-la-Mer for an act of religious worship followed by a fair with horse-racing and bull-fighting. The attraction of the modern town lies in the legend of the arrival of a boat in AD 40, bearing a group of Christians who had been set adrift without oars or sail from Jerusalem. Among those it carried were Mary, mother of the saints James and John, Mary Jacoby, mother of Saint James the younger and sister of the Virgin Mary, and their black servant Sara. All three stayed in the Camargue and built an oratory on the site of a pagan temple. The two Marys were buried there but their bodies were exhumed in 1448 and placed in a shrine in the massive fortified church. Built in the 1100s, this looks more like a keep than a place of worship and still has the well that provided people with water at times of siege.

Now effigies of the two saints in their boat and of Sara, who was adopted by the gypsies as their patron saint, are paraded through the town twice a year. They are then carried into the sea while a bishop blesses the waters. The legend is also perpetuated in the name of the town itself. Just outside the port, the Musée de Boumain is devoted to a series of waxworks showing life in the Camargue.

The next stop is Saint-Gilles, a busy town on the edge of the Camargue which is only a simple 11 km ride north of l'Albaron. The west front of the church here, with its elaborate carvings, is all that is left of an abbey built in the 1100s to replace the original church where Saint Giles was buried. The abbey itself was largely destroyed and its monks murdered during the religious wars of the 1500s. It has a remarkable stone spiral staircase and a crypt containing the saint's tomb. The Hôtel le Saint-Gilloir has a reputation for producing excellent vegetarian dishes. Market days are on Thursday and Saturday.

After Saint-Gilles, you leave the Camargue to strike north. Take time to visit Nîmes. Founded by the Romans, it has had a very stormy history ever since, from being sacked by the Vandals and other barbarian hordes to enduring plagues and local wars. It is a 20 km ride to the north-west, on a road that becomes gradually hillier. Nîmes has given its name to denim (*de Nîmes*), a tribute to the town's clothmakers, although tourism is now one of its main industries, the Roman remains and the fine gardens laid out in the 18th century attracting many visitors.

The Roman amphitheatre is still an arena for blood sports, with bull-fights regularly staged here. Like the similar arena at Arles, it became a fortress and a walled village before being restored to its original use in the last century. There is also a well-preserved Roman temple, the Maison Carrée, which is around 2000 years old. At one time used as a stable, it now houses a museum of antiquities, displaying Roman artefacts and statuary found in the locality.

The Jardin de la Fontaine, created in the 1700s, is a delightful place to walk, with its spring and water gardens. Here, too, the Roman world is not far away, as the garden incorporates the ruins of a Roman temple, where concerts are held in the summer, and the Tour Mange, part of the original Roman fortifications. There is a splendid view from the top, if you still have the energy to ascend the tower once you have climbed up to it. A little outside the town, just past Uchaud to the south-west, you can visit the source from which Perrier water comes.

I find Pont du Gard, 21 km north-east on the N86, irresistible. This aqueduct carrying water 275 metres across the valley of the river Gardon to Nîmes is one of the great feats of Roman engineering. It is extraordinary to think its three levels of arches were created nearly 2000 years ago. A hundred metres from the bridge the Hôtel le Vieux Moulin must surely have one of the best views to be found in all France. The hotel has a private beach from which you can swim in the river. You can also spend an enjoyable day canoeing on the river from Collias upstream. Avignon is only a leisurely day's ride away.

A longer exploration of the Camargue and the *garrigue* country to the west of the Rhône would take you first from

Avignon to Barbentane, a ride of 10 km. Barbentane is a centre for the distribution of fruit and vegetables grown in the region. Attractions include a 14th-century keep and the 17th-century Château de Barbentane, with a fine interior that includes Louis XV and XVI furniture.

From Barbentane, it is 30 km to Arles by way of the D35. On the way you will pass an 18th-century windmill on your left before coming to the beautiful, tree-shrouded, lavender-scented little valley of the abbey of Saint-Michel-de-Frigolet, which was founded in the 900s. The Provençal liqueur frigolet is made here and can be bought in the abbey shop. The town of Tarascon a few kilometres further on is a striking contrast. The marvellous moated castle here was built in the 1100s and faces the ruins of the rival castle of Beaucaire on the opposite bank of the Rhône. English graffiti on some of the walls recall the time it served as a prison. Tarascon is also a port, once noted for a child-eating monster, the Tarasque, which lived in the Rhône. It was eventually subdued by Saint Martha, whose tomb can be seen in the medieval church named after her. A *fête* at the end of June still celebrates her triumph.

From Arles, the tiny village of l'Albaron is a 15 km ride away. Then you cross the Camargue for 30 km to the walled medieval town of Aigues-Mortes. Travel south along the D570 for 11 km and then turn right on to the D58.

Aigues-Mortes is still a small, fortified city, its great walls rising dramatically in the distance as you approach it. Once it was accessible only by a path across the marshes that stretched away on all sides and it takes its name from the numerous salt lagoons that stud the landscape (*aquae mortae* or *eaux mortes*). The tower of Constance was built by Louis IX in 1246, so he would have a proper embarkation point for the 7th Crusade.

In the early years 10,000 people lived here, but the waterway connecting Aigues-Mortes to the sea began to silt up in the 14th century and now there are less than half that number. The delightful stone-built Hostellerie des Ramparts where I like to stay stands within the ancient walls.

Six km to the south across the salt flats is le Grau-du-Roi, a lively old fishing town, standing at the mouth of the channel that connects Aigues-Mortes to the sea. Restaurants here offer a sumptuous *bouillabaisse*. On the way you can visit the vineyards of Listel, where the wine can be tasted and bought. A further 6 km along the D255 from le Grau-du-Roi and you come to a complete contrast: the modern tourist resort of la Grande-Motte, where the futuristic architecture features huge concrete pyramids containing flats and hotels. The town has many camping sites, a marina, a beach well over a kilometre long, a casino and some excellent restaurants.

The next stage is 30 km of mostly easy cycling from Aigues-Mortes back inland. You go north on the D979 for 18 km, turning left on to the D12, which brings you to Sommières. You could make a detour along the way to see the Roman bridge at Villetelle. Sommières is a medieval town that once supported a carpet factory. This has now been transformed into the Auberge du Pont Romain, an imaginative hotel with an excellent restaurant, particularly for those who like traditional French cooking rather than *nouvelle cuisine*. The town itself is delightful, with narrow streets and arcades and a bridge dating from the 1100s. Climb up to the ruined château above the town for a view over the rooftops below. Market day is Saturday. Just north of the town there is a 12th-century château at Villevielle. Some 10 km to the east, along the D40, is the ancient settlement of Oppidum-de-Nages.

Uzès, 40 km away on the D22, is another medieval town where you can still wander in the old narrow streets. It is one of three towns of its period which was chosen to be restored with government grants, and now has an elegant pedestrianized

centre with stone arcades, open squares and smart façades. Its
high Tour Fenestrelle is all that remains of a 12th-century
cathedral that was destroyed by the Huguenots. In a little street
opposite is the Hôtel d'Entraigues, which can be recommended.
Although basically medieval, the town has houses dating from
the 12th to the 18th century, the most interesting of which is Le
Duche, home of the Ducs d'Uzès, a château dating from the
1100s. Jean Racine, one of France's greatest playwrights, lived in
the town in the early 1660s, when seeking advancement from an
influential uncle.

North of Uzès, 17 km along the D979, the clifftop village of
Lussan lies in *garrigue* country, bare limestone hills, carpeted with
gorse, lavender, thyme and rosemary. This wild landscape is cleft
by deep gorges carved through the limestone by the fast-
flowing rivers. To see the most spectacular, turn right on to the
D143 from Lussan and left on to the D643 until you come to the
Aiguillon gorge, cut deep into the rock. In the summer, the river-
bed is dry and you can walk along it.

From Uzès it is a simple 17 km journey along the D981 to
Pont du Gard, and from there an easy ride back to Avignon. It is
worth making a detour from Pont du Gard to see Castillon-du-
Gard, 4 km to the north on the D192. This is yet another
delightful old village with an excellent restaurant.

A more gentle tour of Provence to the north-east of Avignon
could be done in a week, staying at Pernes-les-Fontaines,
Caromb and Venasque. This is a hillier area than the Camargue or
the Rhône valley and it is best to avoid roads crossing the ridges.
Pernes-les-Fontaines is 23 km from Avignon, along the D28. It is
worth making a detour on to the D16 after 15 km to see the
beautiful and colourful formations in the long cave known as the
Grotte de Thouzon. On the brow of the hill that rises above the
cave are the ruins of a château and a monastery. Continue south
for 3 km and you come to le Thor, a small medieval town that is a

distribution centre for the delicious white grapes grown in the area. You can still see the ruined walls of its old fortifications and the ancient bridge across the river Sorgue. Near the bridge is an impressive church dating from the late 13th century.

Pernes-les-Fontaines is yet another old town, known particularly for its 32 fountains, all carefully signposted. Its clock-tower is actually a keep, all that remains of the castle, and there is a tiny chapel on the bridge over the Nesque. The square Ferrande Tower is decorated inside with 700-year-old frescoes. The town has some excellent foodshops, including a *fromagerie* with a fine selection of cheeses. The Hôtel de l'Hermitage is a particularly relaxing place to stay. It is surrounded by a large garden, where you can sit and read, or refresh yourself with a drink after a day on the road.

Caromb is 15 km away. The best route is by the D212 and D938 until you reach Carpentras, turning right on to the D13. Carpentras is charming. Its name derives from the chariots that were once made here, but now it is better known for its sweets—caramels, or *berlingots*. Few signs of its Roman beginnings remain, apart from the triumphal arch. The cathedral of Saint-Siffrein dates from the 1400s, and there is a synagogue of the same period, the oldest in the country and a reminder of a Jewish quarter that probably existed in Roman times. The Palace of Justice, which contains some interesting paintings, was built in the 1600s. Museums include the Sobirats Museum, an 18th-century house displaying furnishings and décor of the period, and the Duplessis Museum, which has a collection of paintings, including some by local artists. Caromb itself is a delightful Provençal hilltop town, built on top of a little pinnacle and centred around an ancient settlement. The Hôtel le Beffroi can be recommended.

North-east of Caromb is the highest peak in Provence, the 2000-metre Mont Ventoux, a wild and windy prominence, capped with snow in winter and early spring and always shining white from the pebbles that gleam on its summit. It is a stiff climb towards the top, but the reward is a stunning panoramic view of Provence and the Rhône valley in all its splendour.

A ride of 15 km south from Caromb brings you to Venasque overlooking the plateau of Vaucluse, once a seat of the archbishops of Comtat. A fairly level ride to this ancient, hilltop village is by the D70 to Mazan and then the D163 and D77 through Malemort-du-Comtat. The baptistry at Venasque, dating back to the 500s, is one of the oldest religious buildings in France. The church of Notre-Dame is also old, first built in the 1100s though altered later. Just outside the town, about 2 km along the D28 and D4, is the Notre-Dame-de-Vie chapel containing the tomb of Bishop Bohetius who died in 604. The Hôtel la Garrigue in Venasque is recommended.

The small town of Gordes, 15 km from Venasque down the scenic D177, rises dramatically in tiers up a rock face. At the top, a renaissance château built on the site of an earlier fortress dominates the town. Part of it is now given over to a museum devoted to the work of the contemporary Hungarian painter Victor Vasarely, noted for his geometrical art. Not far away—go along the D15 for about 3 km, turning right just after the junction with the D2—is the curious *village noir*, a group of the old dry-stone houses known as *bories*, with their steeply-pointed roofs. The village has been inhabited within the last hundred years and is now preserved as a museum of country life.

Another good excursion from Venasque is to see the source of the Sorgue at Fontaine-de-Vaucluse, which is also 15 km away. Go to Saint-Didier along the D28 and then along the D210 and D57. The head-waters of the river come from an emerald-green spring gushing powerfully out of a funnel-shaped cave at the foot of encircling cliffs. Smaller springs have formed a large pool, which is fringed by tall plane trees. In winter and spring, the water flows at a tremendous rate in a foaming fall; in summer, though, it is less spectacular. There is a *son-et-lumière* here from mid June to mid September. The village, with its ruined castle, was the country home of the exiled Italian poet Petrarch (1304–74), who wrote some of his best-known love poems there, inspired by his unrequited passion for Laura, the woman he first saw in 1327 in an Avignon church.

Not far away is l'Isle-sur-la-Sorgue, a small town built on an island in the river Sorgue delightfully girdled by water. Its church has a magnificent 17th-century interior and there is an old hospital with an equally splendid great hall, and an impressive range of pharmacy pots.

You could return to Avignon from Venasque, but for a longer tour of the region next make for Joucas. This is a 15 km ride along the winding little D4 past Murs, turning right on to the D102. From Joucas you can easily explore Gordes, Fontaine-de-Vaucluse and Roussillon, a colourful hilltop village on the highest escarpment separating the Coulon valley and the plateau of Vaucluse. The hills in this area are composed of ochre, which comes in numerous shades of red and yellow and is used to colour the local houses, producing an extraordinary effect that has attracted many painters to the area. There are splendid views from Roussillon over the surrounding countryside. At Joucas the Hostellerie des Commandeurs is a family hotel with wonderful views on the edge of this tiny village. There is a tennis court for those with surplus energy and I have always eaten well here.

It is a ride of some 30 km to Lauris along the D60, D36 and D943. On the way you pass the fortified village of Bonnieux, which has a terrific view across the valley from its 12th-century church, and Lourmarin, dominated by a château—part 15th-century, part renaissance. It is well worth climbing the tower for the view from the top. The village also has an excellent restaurant, le Moulin, which is closed on Mondays. The Hôtel la

Chaumière in Lauris has a lovely situation looking across the valley of the Durance. You can watch the *chef de cuisine* producing spectacular dishes before your eyes, as the kitchen is visible through a glass partition from the dining-room. Market day at Lauris is Monday.

The Abbaye de Silvacane is 9 km to the south across the river, just outside la Roque d'Anthéron. Founded by Cistercian monks in the mid 1100s in the marshes beside the river, it was built over a period of about 400 years. It has had a turbulent history and was abandoned after the Revolution when its vineyards and orchards were destroyed, becoming in turn a church, a refuge for outlaws and a barn before the government recently intervened to restore it to its former glory. It is open most of the year round, although it is closed on Tuesdays. La Roque d'Anthéron to the west is a small town with a 17th-century château at its centre, now used as a convalescent home.

Some 12 km east from Lauris, or 8 km from Lourmarin on the D135, is Ansouis, a village that believes in flaunting what it has. It contains the surprisingly named Musée Extraordinaire, which turns out to be not so extraordinary, although its exhibits include some depicting life under the sea. Just outside the town—go along the D56 for 4 km or so—there is Sabran Castle, a medieval fortress turned into a comfortable manor house that has always been owned by the same family; it contains interesting collections of arms and fine tapestries and there are splendid views from the terraced gardens.

This area is crossed by the mountain range of the Lubéron, which includes a regional park. Scattered near the roadside you will find more examples of *bories*. Some date back before the Roman occupation; others are thought to be of more recent origin and may have served as refuges for townspeople fleeing the epidemics of plague.

The next overnight stop is at la Barben, the village

surrounding the magnificent Château de la Barben, a medieval castle with a small zoo and aquarium in its grounds. The Hôtel la Touloubre, finely situated on the edge of the Trévaresse mountains, has a reputation for excellent food. To get there, cross the river at Cadenet and turn on to the D66 to Lambesc before continuing along the D15. Lambesc is an interesting little town with a 16th-century gateway and a church whose spire collapsed during an earthquake in 1909.

The busy Salon-de-Provence is 6 km away, dominated by Emperi Castle, built on the top of a rock in the 900s and rebuilt over the centuries. It contains a military museum that traces army history until the First World War. The town itself has two medieval churches, Saint-Michel and Saint-Lauren. The latter contains the tomb of the astrologer Nostradamus, whose extraordinary prophecies written in verse in 1555 are still best-sellers today.

About 12 km from Salon (down the D15 from la Barben) is Cornillon-Confoux, a cliffside village overlooking the valley of the river Touloubre. Between it and Grans (well signposted on the D19) is the Hôtel Devem de Mirapier, a new hotel with a tennis court and swimming-pool. Not far away is the Etang de Berre, the shallow lagoon joined to the sea by a canal that is France's main petroleum port. A superb panorama of the *étang* and the hills that ring it can be enjoyed at Lançon, a short ride away from the hotel, where steps lead to a viewing platform.

On the edge of the lagoon, along the D70, is Saint-Chamas, overlooked by an aqueduct built on three arches, one above the other. A little further on is the Pont Flavian over the river Touloubre, named after the Roman who had it constructed more than 1800 years ago.

Just a few kilometres north is Miramas-le-Vieux, another small town built on rock that has the remains of medieval walls. There are also the ruins of an ancient church and a tiny church of the 1100s standing in the grounds of a slightly larger church built 300 years later.

From Cornillon-Confoux it is 35 km to Maussane-les-Alpilles along the D10, D5 and D17. Another 10 km along the D5 takes you to Saint-Rémy-de-Provence, and a further 20 km to Barbentane—take the D5 to Graveson, a large village with an interesting church, and then the N570 and D77. You could stop overnight in Saint-Rémy if you want to go directly back to Avignon.

HOTEL
INFORMATION

1 Mayenne and Sarthe

Chailland
Hôtel des Voyageurs,
53420 Chailland
Tel: (43) 02 70 12

la Chartre-sur-le-Loir
Hôtel de France,
72340 la Chartre-sur-le-Loir
Tel: (43) 44 40 16

Château-Gontier
Hôtel le Parc,
53200 Château-Gontier
Tel: (43) 07 10 80

Entrammes
Hôtel le Lion d'Or,
53260 Entrammes
Tel: (43) 98 30 08

Gorron
Hôtel de Bretagne,
41 Rue de Bretagne,
53120 Gorron
Tel: (43) 04 63 67

Lassay
Auberge du Lassay,
53110 Lassay
Tel: (43) 04 71 61

Luché-Pringé
Auberge du Port des
   Roches,
Luché-Pringé,
72800 le Lude
Tel: (43) 45 44 48

le Lude
Hôtel du Maine,
Route de Saumur,
72800 le Lude
Tel: (43) 94 60 54

Mayenne
Grand Hôtel,
2 Rue Ambroise de Lore,
53100 Mayenne
Tel: (43) 04 37 35

Mézangers
Relais du Gue de Selle,
Mézangers,
53600 Evron
Tel: (43) 90 64 05

Neau
Hôtel de la Croix Verte,
53150 Neau
Tel: (43) 98 23 41

Sablé-sur-Sarthe
Hôtel Saint Martin,
72300 Sablé-sur-Sarthe
Tel: (43) 95 00 03

Saint-Pierre-des-Nids
Hôtel du Dauphin,
53370 Saint-Pierre-des-Nids
Tel: (43) 03 52 12

Saint-Symphorien
Relais de la Charnie,
le Bourg,
Saint-Symphorien,
72480 Bernay-en-Champagne
Tel: (43) 20 72 06

Saulges
Hôtel l'Ermitage,
53340 Saulges
Tel: (43) 01 22 28/65

Solesmes
Grand Hôtel de Solesmes,
Solesmes,
72300 Sablé-sur-Sarthe
Tel: (43) 95 45 10

Vaiges
Hôtel du Commerce,
53480 Vaiges
Tel: (43) 90 50 07

2 Châteaux of the Loire

Bouchemaine
Hôtel l'Ancre de Marine
Bouchemaine,
49000 Angers
Tel: (41) 77 14 46

Chacé
Auberge de Thouet,
Chacé,
49400 Saumur
Tel: (41) 52 97 02

Chinon
Grand Hôtel de la Boule d'Or,
66 Quai Jeanne D'Arc,
37500 Chinon
Tel: (47) 93 03 13

Hôtel Diderot,
7 Rue Diderot,
37500 Chinon
Tel: (47) 93 18 87

Doué-la-Fontaine
Hôtel de France,
49700 Doué-la-Fontaine
Tel: (41) 59 12 27

Fontevraud
Hôtel la Croix Blanche,
49590 Fontevraud
Tel: (41) 51 71 11

Jallais
Hôtel la Croix Verte,
Place de la Mairie,
49510 Jallais
Tel: (41) 64 20 22

Lilette
Auberge de l'Islette,
Lilette,
37160 Descartes
Tel: (47) 59 72 22

Loches
Hôtel George Sand,
39 Rue Quintefol,
37600 Loches
Tel: (47) 59 39 74

Mauléon
Hotel de l'Europe,
15 Rue de l'Hôpital,
79700 Mauléon
Tel: (49) 81 40 33

Montreuil-Bellay
Splendid Hôtel
Rue du Docteur Gaudrez,
49260 Montreuil-Bellay
Tel: (41) 52 35 50

Montsoreau
Hôtel le Bussy,
49730 Montsoreau
Tel: (41) 51 70 18

Oiron
Relais du Château,
Oiron,
79100 Thouars
Tel: (49) 96 51 14

la Roche-Clermault
Auberge du Haut-Clos,
la Roche-Clermault,
37500 Chinon
Tel: (47) 95 94 50

Saint-Jean-de-Thouars
Hôtel du Château,
79100 Saint-Jean-de-Thouars
Tel: (49) 66 18 52/14 62

Saint-Laurent-sur-Sèvre
L'Hermitage Hôtel
Saint-Laurent-sur-Sèvre,
85290 Mortagne-sur-Sèvre
Tel: (51) 67 83 03

Savonnières
Ferme la Martinière,
Savonnières,
37510 Joué-lès-Tours
Tel: (47) 50 04 46

Veigné
Le Moulin Fleuri,
Route de Monts,
37250 Veigné
Tel: (47) 26 01 12

3 La Venise Verte

Celles-sur-Belle
Hôtel le National,
79379 Celles-sur-Belle
Tel: (49) 79 80 34

Chaunay
Hôtel Central,
86510 Chaunay
Tel: (49) 59 25 04

Chenay
Hôtel les Trois Pigeons,
79120 Chenay
Tel: (49) 07 38 59

Coulon
Hôtel le Central,
79510 Coulon
Tel: (49) 35 90 20

Hôtel au Marais,
46–48 Quai Louis-Tardy,
79510 Coulon
Tel: (49) 35 90 43

Gournay
Château des Touches,
79110 Gournay
Tel: (49) 29 31 23

Maillezais
Hostellerie Saint-Nicolas,
85420 Maillezais
Tel: (51) 00 74 45

Olbreuse
Château d'Olbreuse,
Mauzé-sur-le-Mignon,
79210 Olbreuse
Tel: (49) 04 85 74

Saint-Maixent-l'Ecole
Auberge du Cheval Blanc,
8 Avenue Gambetta,
79400 Saint-Maixent-l'Ecole
Tel: (49) 05 50 06

Saint-Romans-lès-Melle
Chambres d'Hôte,
Saint-Romans-lès-Melle,
79500 Melle
Tel: (49) 27 04 15

Villiers-en-Bois
Auberge des Cedres,
Villiers-en-Bois,
79360 Beauvoir-sur-Niort
Tel: (49) 09 60 53

4 Cognac and the Dordogne

Aubeterre-sur-Dronne
Hôtel du Périgord
16390 Aubeterre-sur-
Dronne
Tel: (45) 98 50 11

Auberge du Château,
9 Place du Château,
16390 Aubeterre-sur-
Dronne
Tel: (45) 98 50 46

Barbezieux
Hôtel la Boule d'Or,
9 Boulevard Gambetta,
16300 Barbezieux
Tel: (45) 78 22 72/3

Brossac
Chambres d'Hôte,
Place de l'Eglise,
16480 Brossac
Tel: (45) 98 71 50

Fleurac
Château de Fleurac,
Fleurac,
16200 Jarnac
Tel: (45) 81 78 22

Mareuil-sur-Belle
Auberge du Moulin
Fontverte,
24340 Mareuil-sur-Belle
Tel: (53) 60 96 77

Montbron
Hôtel des Trois
Marchands,
Place du Cedre,
16220 Montbron
Tel: (45) 70 71 29

Nontron
Grand Hôtel Pélisson,
Place Alfred Agard,
24300 Nontron
Tel: (53) 56 11 22

la Rochefoucauld
La Vieille Auberge,
16110 la Rochefoucauld
Tel: (45) 62 02 72

Roumazières-Loubert
Hôtel du Commerce,
Route de la Gare,
16270 Roumazières-Loubert
Tel: (45) 71 21 38

Saint-Groux
Hôtel les Trois Saules,
Saint-Groux,
16230 Mansle
Tel: (45) 20 31 40

Verteuil
Hôtel la Paloma,
Route de Villars,
16510 Verteuil
Tel: (45) 31 41 32

Vibrac
Hôtel les Ombrages,
Vibrac,
16120 Châteauneuf
Tel: (45) 97 32 33

Vieux-Mareuil
Auberge de l'Etang Bleu,
Vieux-Mareuil,
24340 Mareuil
Tel: (53) 60 92 63

**5 Bordeaux and
Garonne**

Agen
Hostellerie de la Rigalette,
47000 Agen
Tel: (53) 47 37 44

Aiguillon
Hôtel les Cygnes,
47190 Aiguillon
Tel: (53) 79 60 02

Allemans-du-Dropt
Hôtel l'Etape Gascogne,
47800 Allemans-du-Dropt
Tel: (53) 20 23 55

Bon-Encontre
Hôtel le Parc,
41 Rue de la Republique,
47240 Bon-Encontre
Tel: (53) 96 17 75

Casseneuil
Auberge la Résidence,
47440 Casseneuil
Tel: (53) 41 08 08

Casteljaloux
Hôtel aux Cadets de
Gascogne,
Place Gambetta,
47700 Casteljaloux
Tel: (53) 93 00 59

Duras
Hostellerie des Ducs,
47120 Duras
Tel: (53) 83 74 58

Monbazillac
Relais de la Diligence,
Route d'Eymet,
Monbazillac,
24240 Sigoules
Tel: (53) 58 30 48

Moncrabeau
Hôtel le Phare,
Moncrabeau,
47600 Nérac
Tel: (53) 65 42 08

Monflanquin
Le Moulin de Boulède,
Route de Cancon,
47150 Monflanquin
Tel: (53) 36 40 27

Monpazier
Hôtel de France,
21 Rue Saint-Jacques,
24540 Monpazier
Tel: (53) 22 60 06/66 01

Nérac
Hôtel Restaurant d'Albret,
40, 42 Allées d'Albret,
47600 Nérac
Tel: (53) 65 01 47

Hôtel du Château,
7 Avenue de Mondenard,
47600 Nérac
Tel: (53) 65 09 05

Sainte-Livrade-sur-Lot
Hôtel le Midi,
47110 Sainte-Livrade-sur-Lot
Tel: (53) 01 00 32

Saussignac
Relais de Saussignac,
Saussignac,
24240 Sigoules
Tel: (53) 27 92 08

Tombeboeuf
Hôtel du Nord,
Tombeboeuf,
47380 Monclar
Tel: (53) 88 83 15

Villefranche-du-Périgord
Hôtel les Bruyères,
Route de Cahors,
24550 Villefranche-du-
Périgord
Tel: (53) 29 97 97

Villeréal
Hostellerie du Lac,
47210 Villeréal
Tel: (53) 36 01 39

6 Beaujolais and Jura

Anse
Hôtel Saint-Romain,
Route de Graves,
69480 Anse
Tel: (74) 68 05 89

Arinthod
Hôtel de la Tour,
39240 Arinthod
Tel: (84) 48 00 05

Ars-sur-Formans
Grand Hôtel de la Basilique,
Ars,
01480 Jassans-Riottier
Tel: (74) 00 73 76

Bourg-Saint-Christophe
Hôtel Chez Ginette,
01800 Bourg Saint-
Christophe
Tel: (74) 61 01 49

Ceyzériat
Hôtel Mont July,
01250 Ceyzériat
Tel: (74) 30 00 12

Châtillon-sur-Chalaronne
Au Chevalier Norbert,
01400 Châtillon-sur-
Chalaronne
Tel: (74) 55 02 22

Corcelles-en-Beaujolais
Hôtel Gailleton,
69220 Belleville
Tel: (74) 66 41 06

Cuiseaux
Hôtel du Commerce,
71480 Cuiseaux
Tel: (85) 72 71 79

Hôtel du Nord,
71480 Cuiseaux
Tel: (85) 72 71 02

Lachassagne
Au Goutillon Beaujolais,
69480 Lachassagne
Tel: (74) 67 14 99

Louhans
Hôtel du Cheval Rouge,
5 Rue d'Alsace,
71500 Louhans
Tel: (85) 75 21 42

Meximieux
Hôtel Lutz,
01800 Meximieux
Tel: (74) 61 06 78

Montmerle-sur-Saône
Hôtel du Rivage,
01140 Thoissey
Tel: (74) 69 33 92

Orgelet
Hôtel de la Valouse,
39270 Orgelet
Tel: (84) 25 40 64

Pont-de-Poitte
Hôtel de l'Ain,
39130 Clairvaux-les-Lacs
Tel: (84) 48 30 16

Romenay
Hôtel du Lion d'Or,
71470 Montpont
Tel: (85) 40 30 78

Saint-Amour
Hôtel d'Alliance,
39160 Saint-Amour
Tel: (84) 48 74 94

Sainte-Croix
Hôtel Chez Nous,
01120 Sainte-Croix
Tel: (78) 06 17 92

Salles-en-Beaujolais
Hostellerie Saint-Vincent,
69460 Salles-en-Beaujolais
Tel: (74) 67 55 50

Sarcey
Hôtel Chatard,
69490 Sarcey
Tel: (74) 01 20 01

7 The Rhone Valley

Alixan
Hôtel de France,
26300 Alixan
Tel: (75) 47 03 44

Arthémonay
Auberge le Pont du Chalon,
26260 Saint-Donat-sur-
l'Herbasse
Tel: (75) 45 62 13

Crest
Grand Hôtel,
Rue de l'Hôtel de Ville,
26400 Crest
Tel: (75) 25 08 17

Génissieux
Hôtel la Chaumière,
26750 Génissieux
Tel: (75) 02 77 97

Grane
Hôtel Giffon,
26400 Crest,
Grane
Tel: (75) 62 60 64/70 11

Grange-les-Beaumont
Hôtel Restaurant Lanaz,
26600 Granges-les-
Beaumont
Tel: (75) 71 50 56

Hauterives
Hôtel Restaurant le Relais
26390 Hauterives
Tel: (75) 68 81 12

Mirmande
Hôtel la Capitelle,
Le Rampart,
26270 Mirmande
Tel: (75) 63 02 72

Pélussin
Hôtel de l'Ancienne Gare,
42410 Pélussin
Tel: (74) 87 61 51

Peyrus
Hôtel du Commerce et
du Parc,
26120 Chabeuil
Tel: (75) 59 80 08

Saint-Jean-de-Bournay
Grand Hôtel du Nord,
38440 Saint-Jean-de-
Bournay
Tel: (74) 58 52 25

Saint-Vallier
Hôtel des Voyageurs,
2 Avenue Jean Jaures,
26240 Saint-Vallier
Tel: (75) 23 04 42

Tournon
Hôtels de Paris/du Château,
Quai Marc Sequin,
07300 Tournon
Tel: (75) 08 60 22

Tullins
Auberge de Malatras,
38210 Tullins
Tel: (76) 07 02 30

Viriville
Hôtel Bonnoit,
38980 Viriville
Tel: (74) 54 02 18

la Voulte-sur-Rhône
Hôtel le Musée,
Place du 4 Septembre,
07800 la Voulte-sur-Rhône
Tel: (75) 62 40 19

8 Provence

Aigues Mortes
Hostellerie des Ramparts,
Place Anatole France,
30220 Aigues Mortes
Tel: (66) 53 82 77

l'Albaron
Hôtel le Flamant Rose,
13123 Albaron
Tel: (90) 97 10 18

Arles
Hôtel d'Arlatan,
26 Rue Sauvage,
13200 Arles
Tel: (90) 93 53 66

la Barben
Hôtel la Touloubre,
13330 la Barben
Tel: (90) 55 16 85

Caromb
Hôtel le Beffroi,
84330 Caromb
Tel: (90) 62 45 63

Cornillon-Confoux
Hôtel Devem de Mirapier,
13250 Saint-Chamas
Tel: (90) 55 99 22

Joucas
Hostellerie des Commandeurs,
84220 Gordes
Tel: (90) 72 00 05

Lauris
Hôtel la Chaumière,
Place du Portail,
84360 Lauris
Tel: (90) 68 01 29

Maussane-les-Alpilles
Hôtel l'Oustaloun,
Place de l'Eglise,
13520 Maussane les Alpilles
Tel: (90) 97 32 19

Morières-lès-Avignon
Hotel le Paradou,
Avenue Leon Blum,
84310 Morières-lès-Avignon
Tel: (90) 22 35 85

Pernes-les-Fontaines
Hôtel de l'Hermitage,
Route de Carpentras,
84210 Pernes-les-Fontaines
Tel: (90) 66 51 41

Pont du Gard
Hôtel le Vieux Moulin,
30210 Remoulins
Tel: (66) 37 14 35

Saint-Rémy-de-Provence
Le Chalet Fleuri,
Avenue Frédéric-Mistral,
13210 Saint-Rémy-de-
Provence
Tel: (90) 92 03 62

Saint-Gilles
Hôtel le Saint-Gilloir,
30800 Saint-Gilles
Tel: (66) 87 33 69

Sommières
Auberge du Pont Romain,
2 Rue Emile Jamais,
30250 Sommières
Tel: (66) 80 00 58

Uzès
Hôtel d'Entraigues,
8 Rue de la Calade,
30700 Uzès
Tel: (66) 22 32 68

Venasque
Hôtel la Garrigue,
Route de Murs,
Venasque,
84210 Pernes-les-Fontaines
Tel: (90) 66 03 40

INDEX